alligators under my bed
and other nebraska tales

James D. Hager
a memoir

TROY, OHIO

Cover Illustration by Sveta Eremenko.
Illustration copyright © 2009 Clay Bridges Communications & Publishing

Author Photograph by Sharon Elaine Photography, Tipp City, Ohio.
Copyright released 2009 © Clay Bridges Communications & Publishing.

Interior family photographs provided by family members and used with permission,
unless otherwise noted. All photographs precede 1976 Copyright Act regulations.

Historical photographs and charts are from yearbooks and public documents preceding
the 1976 Copyright Act regulations and/or contain no copyright information, with the
exception of the following pictures: Maynard Hospital, page 42; Red Cloud parade,
page 110; Potter building fire, page 174; and Lincoln School, page 104. These four
pictures were approved for publication by Harriett Yost Zade, the editor of the Red
Cloud Chief newspaper, and were originally found in the book *Red Cloud, Nebraska a
History in Pictures*. Our thanks to those who photographically documented this time and
place in history.

Photos © Walker Studio. Pages 7, 67, 101
Photos © Jim Hager. Pages 11, 62, 72, 92, 157

Copyright © 2009 James D. Hager. All rights reserved.

No part of this publication may be reproduced, stored in a retrieval system, or transmitted
in any form or by any means—electronic, mechanical, photocopy, recording, or any other—
except for brief quotations in printed reviews, without the prior permission of the publisher or
as may be expressly permitted by the 1976 Copyright Act.

Requests for information, copyright permissions, or comments should be addressed to:
Clay Bridges Communications & Publishing, 300 South Ridge Avenue, Troy, Ohio,
45373 or *info@claybridges.com*.

Alligators Under My Bed And Other Nebraska Tales
is a Clay Bridges Communications & Publishing publication.

Clay Bridges seeks to provide resources and education to build up people to span life's
circumstances. For speaking, training, or author events, visit www.*ClayBridges.com* or
contact us at the information listed above.

Library of Congress Control Number: 2009931259
ISBN: 978-0-9819807-2-0

Printed and Manufactured in the United States of America

a tribute

In my forty-six years of college and business experience, I have taken courses and provided training in business ethics and leadership. Those training experiences were never more important, or as profound, as the coaching and mentoring I received in my years in the Red Cloud School System and working for the business leaders described in this autobiography of my youth. As I made good choices and poor choices through my career, my values, beliefs, and principles of business came from people like Ernie Warner, Marvin Jones, Orville Miksch, and other community leaders in Red Cloud. Of course, my Christian faith was paramount for my getting through the highs and lows of life and traveling the right paths.

- Jim Hager

To: Sharon Miller

From: Darrell Kirstine

2-25-2014

table of contents

The Philosophical Introduction.................................. 5

1	The Necessary History.................................. 7
2	The Family Takes Root............................... 14
3	The Birth of a Nebraska Boy....................... 17
4	The Tough, Early Years............................... 19
5	The Memories of Boyhood.......................... 25
6	The Big Move to a New Farm...................... 36
7	District 26—The Bohemian School.............. 44
8	The Rural Farming Lifestyle........................ 54
9	Trips to Town.. 67
10	Big Changes on the Farm............................ 74
11	Big Changes for a Nebraska Boy.................. 96
12	A New Beginning in Red Cloud.................. 104
13	The Middle School Years............................ 134
14	A Nebraska High Schooler.......................... 153
15	Senior Year: The Nebraska Boy Grown Up... 177

Epilogue: The Rest of the Story................................ 190
Endnotes.. 193
Acknowledgements.. 195
Works Cited... 197

the philosophical introduction

All the experiences of youth are stored in the convolutions of the brain and mesh to form our character. Faith, values, and beliefs become our perception of truth. Certain principles and morals manifest certain choices and behaviors. Fears appear at times, seemingly for no reason. Humor pops out in the presence of awkward moments. Love blossoms into flowers—or weeds.

Character is like the keel of a boat. The keel keeps the boat on course. It is laid before the boat is built. Without a keel, a boat wanders across the water without direction. The slightest wind or wave against a keelless boat changes its course. The straightness of the keel determines the strength of the boat.

So it is, that our youthful experiences create the character that takes its course through life. Responsible adults nurture and mentor the youth of their day, and thus lay the keel for the next generation's character.

This book is about my life, growing up in a little, rural town in the center of the original 48 states. Many adults nurtured and mentored me to become the character that I am.

To learn more about this character, read on. Someone might want to know about the life of a boy who grew up in Nebraska. Members of my family may want to know more about their heritage. Grandkids may want to know what times were like when their grandpa grew up. My friends may want to see why I turned out the way I did. Historians may want to know about living in the USA during the mid-twentieth century. Libraries may want to store information about individual lives for future generations. Sociologists may want to study the cultural influence of rural living on family and on vocational outcomes. Psychologists may want to study the psychological impact of a rural upbringing. And some may be curious about the details of another life—to avoid some of the pitfalls, gain wisdom and knowledge, or simply pass the time reading about a boy from Nebraska.

An autobiography is a story of one's life written by one's self. The following details are from memory. So maybe instead, I am writing my memoir. A memoir is considered to be a record of happenings based on the writer's personal observation and knowledge of special information. Whether autobiography or memoir, this writing is about James David Hager as remembered by the same. The beauty of a memoir is that no one can refute it. It is my memory of the way things happened or stories told to me by my family. I promise to do my best to be as accurate as my memory serves me (as old age allows). And, I will try not to unnecessarily tell someone else's story as my own.

chapter one
the necessary history

My roots are in the soil of south central Nebraska, near the Republican River. If one were to look at the flat bottom part of Nebraska, excluding the panhandle, the Republican River flows from the west into the Harlan County Lake and continues east along the Nebraska border just south of Red Cloud. Webster County was the home of my youth. The south side of Webster County borders the state of Kansas. Red Cloud, the county seat, is my hometown. The Burlington & Missouri River Railroad line is just south of town, running east and west. Red Cloud is also the junction of two highways: Highway 136, which runs east and west, and Highway 281, which runs north and south.

By now, you may have noticed there are a lot of directions mentioned. In the Midwest, the land is laid out in north/south and east/west plots. Midwesterners usually do not give directions such as left or right. Rather, they use compass ordinals—north, south, east, or west.

Midwest History

Before there were states and counties west of the Missouri River, this harsh, disorganized territory lay in the heart of the

Great Plains. In 1803, President Jefferson purchased approximately 800,000 square miles of land from the French for about fifteen million dollars. The land was called the Louisiana Purchase. The Louisiana Purchase doubled the size of the United States. As far as the eye could see, the land was an endless sea of prairie grass, large rivers, and vast herds of buffalo.

Adventurous pioneers, many of whom were immigrants, traveled the 2,000 mile Oregon Trail during the mid 1800s through the middle of this untamed land. They started from towns like Independence, St. Louis, and St. Joseph, Missouri. Wagon trains traveled along the Little Blue River to the Platt River and out to the western part of the United States' territory. Other wagon trains traveled the Platt River from Old Fort Kearney and Council Bluffs, Iowa to join the Oregon Trail. West of the Continental Divide, many pioneers settled in what is now Nevada and California.

As wagons broke down and desperation set in, some pioneers stayed on the prairie. In order to survive, they had to bust up the sod for farm land, build homes, and establish towns, which supplied the wagon trains, replenished livestock, provided repairs, and were a safe haven for those who dared to keep heading west. The U.S. Government established forts for military protection. One such fort was Fort Kearney, near the Platt River. Other forts were established along the Oregon Trail every 200 to 400 miles. Wagon wheel ruts along the Oregon Trail can still be seen in areas undisturbed by the plow.

The indigenous populations, commonly referred to as Native American Indians, were a great threat to settlers, the US Army, and the growth of the nation as it moved west. The Indians disliked the encroaching settlements of white populations and the changes they brought. The westward growth of the nation was also a great threat to Native Americans, resulting in the loss of their livelihood and their access to land and life-sustaining resources.

Pawnee Indians, the largest Native American Indian tribe in the region, lived in villages along the rivers of what is now central Nebraska and northern Kansas. The Republican

Pawnee Tribe had a number of permanent tribal villages along the Republican River in what is now Webster County, Nebraska. The Pawnee farmed seasonal crops and hunted the vast herds of buffalo from the western plains to the Rocky Mountains.

In the early 1800s, the conflict between other northwest Indian Nations of the Great Plains and the US Government, and the westward settlements of white people, pushed the Pawnees into southern Kansas and Oklahoma.

Nebraska History

In 1854, the Kansas-Nebraska Act was created to establish the territories of Kansas and Nebraska. The Act opened the land west of the Missouri River to settlement, dealt with slavery issues, and made provisions for the transcontinental railroad development. Then the government created the Homestead Act of 1862 to give free land to those who would settle the western territories of America.

The Homestead Act of 1862 deeded land to any family head or twenty-one-year-old US citizen. Homesteaders were required to live on the land for five years and improve the property with a house, barn, trees, and crops. Upon meeting certain conditions, homesteaders received a quarter section of land (160 acres). Other Federal Acts allowed settlers to purchase 160 acres of land for $1.25 an acre or to receive a quarter section of land in exchange for planting trees on a set number of acres and tending to the land for a certain number of years. All these Acts by the US Government were meant to encourage settlers to occupy the lands of the Great Plains, the Rocky Mountains, and the West.

In addition, as an incentive to build the railroad and to have the means to maintain the rail lines and equipment, the Federal Government granted railroad companies large blocks of land near the rail lines that were to be established. Settlers were encouraged to purchase the Railroad Land Grant sections of land near the rail lines and towns that had rail sidings and depots located in those towns. As a result of these government incentives, the railroads grew rapidly.

After the Civil War in 1867, Nebraska became the 37th state with Lincoln as its capitol. The new State was divided into ninety-three counties.

Webster County History

Webster County, named after Daniel Webster, was established in 1871. Webster County was rich with opportunities. The Republican River valley ran through the southern part of the county, The Burlington & Missouri River Railroad was eventually built along the north side of the county, a north and south line ran down through the middle of the county and an east and west line ran along the Republican River valley. The land in Webster County consisted of rolling hills and creek beds, where run-off water flowed toward the Republican River. Cottonwood trees followed the creek beds and along the river bottom.

The sky was large, and constantly changing weather patterns traveled from west to east across the Great Plains. In the spring and fall, large bird migrations traveled across the grain-abundant land. The seasons changed the land from green to golden browns, to shades of gray, and finally to snow white.

In Webster County, the earliest pioneer homes were dugouts. Later, settlers built log cabins and frame houses. Over time, they converted the Great Plains' prairie grassland into farmland. Eventually, they established towns in the Republican River valley and along the expanding rail lines in the northern part of the County.

Red Cloud History

Silas Garber, who was twice elected Governor of Nebraska, founded Red Cloud in 1871. Serving as the county seat and hosting the thriving railroad gave the town of Red Cloud identity and purpose.

The town's namesake is Chief Red Cloud of the Oglala Sioux nation. Chief Red Cloud was born in 1821 at Bluewater Creek in western Nebraska. In his early years, the young warrior Red Cloud fought aggressively against other Indian tribes, "the white man," and the US Army. He held war councils in many areas of western Nebraska. Red Cloud evolved from warrior to Chief statesman. He was a diplomat in the final treaties between the Sioux Indians and the US Government, which greatly affected the development of the western Great Plains areas. Red Cloud, Nebraska is the only town named after Chief Red Cloud. He was elected to the Nebraska Hall of Fame in the year 2000.

The town of Red Cloud (which is located just 21 miles north of the exact center of the United States—pre-Hawaii and -Alaska) grew as each decade passed. Major banks were established. A number of large two and three story brick commercial buildings were built. Churches and parks sprung up around town. The new County Courthouse and Jail were built. Horse drawn, rail trolley cars ran from the Depot to the center of town. A new Opera House created a grand social and cultural atmosphere. Schools were built for all levels of primary education. Homes for all levels of economic status were built along a north/south/east/west grid of streets. An electrical power plant and telephone system was fully designed and built for the growing little city in south central Nebraska.

Webster Street, 2002

When I was growing up near and in Red Cloud, the population was about 1,575. The town was a shipping center for grain and livestock, both by rail and by truck. Highways 136 (East and West) and 281 (North and South) crossed in the center of town. Red bricks surfaced the highways for two city blocks in all four directions. For the years that I can recall, a single yellow blinking light welcomed the town visitors to slow down at the intersection of Highways 136 and 281. The ever-present Red Cloud town police car sat at the northwest corner of the same intersection.

The little Midwest town had two or three businesses for everything from banks to law offices, from groceries to farm equipment dealerships, from pool halls to drug stores. Like all small towns, it had its schools, volunteer fire station, and post office. For medical needs, there were two doctors, a hospital, a nursing home, two funeral parlors, and some cemeteries. The town had a variety of sports fields, a tennis court, a swimming pool, a movie theater, and later a bowling alley. Most denominations had a church somewhere in town. One block behind the post office was an auction barn for the sale of livestock. Near the railroad tracks were stockyards, grain elevators, petroleum and natural gas storage facilities, and of course, the Burlington & Missouri River Railroad Depot. A golf course and an airstrip were to the east of town. Most of the homes in Red Cloud were to the west of Highway 281, but a smaller number of homes were located to the east, because Crooked Creek, lined with Cottonwood trees, wrapped around the town on the east side.

Out in the country, each farm had an assortment of sheds, grain storage bins, barns, tractors, trucks, and other farm machinery. Oftentimes, the farm dogs ran to bark at the few cars that traveled down the country roads. The landscape, as far as one's eyes could see, was covered with crops of grasses, hay, corn, wheat, and other grains. Cattle and horses were seen roaming the pastures. Cattle paths cut across the pastures, all of which funneled to the gate leading to each farm's barnyard. Miles of fence lines filled with weeds and brush ran next to the roads, along with power lines, for those farms lucky enough to have been electrified. Some highways were paved. Most county roads, with mail and school bus routes, were graveled. Other minor country roads were just plain dirt.

Farm Life History

In the Midwest, land was surveyed and divided into sections of land a mile square, which equals 640 acres. Crows flying high saw the land as a patchwork of sections of land. The patchwork appearance resulted from fields with different crops such as hay, grass, corn, wheat, and oats interspersed with freshly plowed soil. The patchwork terrain looked stitched together by the roads and driveways entering the farmyards.

In the 1940s, farms were located on the sections of land according to how the sections were subdivided. Most often there were two or three farms on a section of land. Each farm might work 640 acres/a full section, 320 acres/a half section, or 160 acres/a quarter section. Successful farmers bought the parts of the section of land that could produce the most grain, hay, or livestock. Black soil was best. Sandy or clay soil was avoided and mostly used as pasture land. In the 40s and 50s, dry-land farming was the norm. Irrigation was not yet available in this part of the country. Farmers just had to pray for regular rains and no hail.

More acres on a farm meant more machinery and buildings. As one drove around the countryside, it was easy to see who had a quarter section of land or a full section of land just by the number of buildings and machines. Small farms had a house, a barn, several small buildings like a chicken coop and a privy (outside toilet), a windmill, a car or pickup, and a tractor. Medium-sized farms had all the above plus chicken houses, a farm equipment maintenance building, and an extra tractor. The large farms added tall feed silos, additional barns, grain storage bins, several large tractors, a combine, a corn picker, and a farm truck.

Farming with horses was on the wane. Tractors were on the move. John Deere, Farmalls, Alis-Chalmers, Olivers, Fords, and International Harvesters were the most common tractors in our area. Every farm had a display of machinery to till and harvest the land. Some were shiny and new; some were well used; and some were abandoned in the weeds and grass, having served the land with purpose.

chapter two
the family takes root

My family roots came from farmer stock. My ancestors were from European and Slovakian descent: French, English, German, and Bohemian. Religious torment, famine, factional conflict, and the dreams of coming to the New World Colonies were reason enough to travel across the Atlantic Ocean to America. My Hager Grandparents, David William (Bill) and Ollie Hager, lived on a farm near Lawrence.

Wilma, Jesse, Frances, Cecil

Fred (Paul) and Hazel (Mary)

On November 11, 1917, my father, Jesse William Hager, the oldest of five children, was born at home. Jesse went to school through the eighth grade.

My grandparents on the Thayer side of my family tree lived in Grand Island, Nebraska. My mother was born as the sixth of thirteen children on July 15, 1917 with the birth name of Mary Olive Thayer. In 1921, Mary and her brother, Paul (the seventh child) were placed in an orphanage in Lincoln, along with three other siblings. In 1922, Mary and Paul were fostered out to James and Carrie Hesman at their farm in Pauline. On April 24, 1924, James and Carrie Hesman adopted Mary and Paul. The adopted siblings names were changed to Hazel and Fred Hesman.

Hazel and Fred were raised on a farm in the Pauline area of Nebraska. Hazel went to school through the eighth grade.

The Family Beginnings

Jesse and Hazel met each other at a July 4, 1935 celebration in Lawrence, Nebraska. Lawrence, a tiny railroad town, was located just east of the Webster county line inside Nuckolls County on Highway 4. For miles around, the tall railroad elevators and the huge Catholic Church could be seen upon approaching the little village. To the west of Lawrence was a tiny cemetery in which generations of Hagers had been and would be laid to rest.

My mom said that she met my dad while sitting on the front fender of a car to watch a parade. He joined her by sitting on the other fender of the car. Their first date was on my mom's 18th birthday. Jesse and Hazel were married in Hastings, Nebraska on February 20, 1937. My mother's full name became Hazel Mary Olive Thayer Hesman Hager.

Early on my parent's lived in Henry, Nebraska, right on the Wyoming-Nebraska border, where my brother, Kenneth Wayne Hager, was born at home on July 17, 1938. Three miles away in Morrill, my sister, Barbara Maxine Hager, was born at home on January 15, 1940. My dad was a farm laborer at the time.

While Barbara was a baby, my parents moved to Riverton, Wyoming. They lived in a small shed-like house and were very poor. Dad worked on a fox farm in Riverton feeding the foxes and fixing the fences where the foxes tried to dig out. The winter was harsh. The young family suffered in that climate.

In 1941, the westward pull of the Oregon Trail took my parents and their two children, Kenneth and Barbara, to Cloverdale, Oregon. Dad worked on a dairy farm located near the Pacific Ocean. My dad told stories about the salmon runs from the ocean up into the small rivers on the Oregon Coast. There were so many fish that he could stand on the river bank and pitchfork salmon to take home for the family. Later, the Hager family moved away from the coast to Albany, Oregon.

In early 1943, my Hager grandparents asked Dad to return to Nebraska to work on their rented farm, which was two miles north and two-and-a-half miles east of Red Cloud, in the Pleasant Hill Precinct, on the SW corner of Section 20. My grandparents wanted to retire and move into their new home on the south end of Red Cloud. Once again, my parents traveled along the Oregon Trail. But this time, they were heading back to Nebraska with a surprise tucked away.

chapter three
the birth of a nebraska boy

My mom told me that while living in Albany, Oregon, they lived in the Nebraska Apartments. It was there that I was conceived. Since I believe life begins at conception, maybe I am an Oregonian born in Nebraska, or because they lived in the Nebraska Apartments, maybe that counts as Nebraska. Either way, it seems that I was fated to have a dual existence as a Nebraskan and an Oregonian.

Many times my mother told the story of my birth as follows:

> It was August 24, 1943, a normal Tuesday on the farm north of Red Cloud. The family canned corn all morning, and in the afternoon they were going to Sale Day in town. However, labor began. They sent for Dr. Obert, the Red Cloud town doctor. The baby would not wait for the doctor. He came into the world twenty minutes before the doctor arrived.
>
> A healthy baby boy was born in the front bedroom of the small farmhouse, with the help of Grandma Ollie Hager at 3:30PM. This bedroom was the same bedroom where my cousins Ronnie and Waunie Lee were born.
>
> The men went to Sale Day anyway and then celebrated a little too much. Mom complained each time she told this story that their going was "not a good idea." When Barbara and Kenneth were brought in to see their new baby brother, Kenneth exclaimed, "Who's that bawlin'?"
>
> The next day the two grandfathers sat in the room with the new mom and baby, James David Hager,

named for both grandfathers: James William Hesman and David William Hager. Mom always appreciated the two grandpas staying there that first day.

That is the story of my birth. The State of Nebraska settled my citizenship. According to my birth certificate, I am officially a Nebraska boy!

My mom was 26 when I was born. She said she did not want any more children after my sister, Barbara. She thought two children were enough for them to take care of. Times were really tough for the young family. There was no need for another child. But my dad's friends and family encouraged him to go ahead and have more kids. Dad agreed. I guess I was the result. While I created a greater burden for the family, I am certain that I brought a lot of joy to them. Mom said many times that she was glad that I came along. When thinking about her childhood experience, one can see why she would fear having more children than she and Dad could support. Being the youngest child, I always felt an older brother and sister were plenty of siblings to bear.

chapter four
the tough early years

In October of 1943, my Hager grandparents moved into Red Cloud to start their retirement.

My parents were left on their own to learn about and to endure the hard life of farming rented land. While I do not remember much of those early years, my mom told me many times that I was sickly. I had convulsions to the point that she thought I would die. Life on this little farm was difficult. After paying the landlord the agreed upon rent, there was not much money left. Dad farmed with two workhorses. They had a few cows and chickens. To farm, they used broken down, horse pulled farm equipment. Extra money they had came from selling cream and eggs when they made their trek to town. They had no electricity and only well water supplied by a windmill near the house.

First Fall/Winter

No wonder I was sickly. Mom told me that when corn was picked, I was laid on the wagon seat in swaddling blankets while they hand picked the corn that first fall. The horses moved down the rows of corn slowly. My parents pulled the ears of corn off the stock, hand shucked the corn, and threw the ears of corn into the wagon. When they were tired or the wagon was full, we all made our way back to the house. I was cold and blue by the end of the day. Mom put me near the cob-burning cook stove to get heat back into my body. Once a week that winter, when the snow was deep enough that the car could not travel the country roads, the family sat in the back of the open wagon while my dad drove the horses across the snowy fields into town. My parents sold their cream and eggs and bought any supplies they could afford.

Then, we traveled back to the farm in the open wagon. Obviously, I made it through that first winter, but just barely.

First Escape

The farm was set on a hill along a dirt road traveling east and west. There were a few trees and some farm equipment sitting wherever they were last used. There were a few run-down buildings: the house, the chicken coop, a privy (outhouse), and the barn. Down the hill, to the west, ran a creek (Dry Creek) lined with cottonwood trees. In the summer, my family picnicked along the creek in the shade, and the kids played in the shallow pools of water. Another family lived just below our house along the creek.

One day, as a toddler, I was missing. Mom became frantic, not finding me in the usual places. Apparently, I had taken a quarter mile hike down to the creek. I lost one of my shoes on the road, so Mom fearfully and correctly suspected I went to the creek. As she made her way down the hill, she saw a tractor coming up the dirt road. I was on the lap of the neighbor who found me. He was bringing me back home.

First Car

As a toddler, I played just outside the front door of the house. The house had a small porch with steps. Along the side of the house was a small mound of dirt held there with stacked boards and a small tree that provided some shade. That was where I kept myself entertained on days with nice weather. I had a toy metal jeep that I moved across the roads I made in the dirt. Sometimes I tried to climb the scraggly little tree. We had a dog that chased cars going by, but I do not remember his name. Farm cats were always around the barn to catch mice and snakes. The dog and cats were my outside playmates.

First Home

Inside the tiny house, the rooms were bare. The house was hot in the summer and freezing in the winter. Each room was wallpapered in various flower patterns with stains of unknown origins. Each room had worn linoleum covering painted wood floors. The house was often dark because we only had kerosene lamps; one or two flames from the lamps made eerie, wiggly yellow patterns on the walls. The two bedrooms contained battered dresser drawers, maybe a chair, and an iron bed that in the winter was piled with blankets or quilts that my grandmother made, or in the summer was covered with just sheets. A thunder pot was kept under the bed in case someone did not want to go outside to the privy at night.

The kitchen had a painted, round leaf table and mismatched pressed back chairs. There were a few cabinets, a dry sink, an icebox, a cob-stove, and a box for cobs. Boots and shoes huddled around the stove. A curled yellow sticky tape hung from the ceiling to catch flies and other flying bugs. On the farm, flies were everywhere, including on our supper. The living room was sparse, with a trampled sofa, a couple chairs, and the fuel oil stove. During bad weather, a wooden rack filled with underclothes absorbed the heat off the stove. In several dark niches, a mousetrap laid, waiting for its prey. Since I was the one playing on the floor, I usually was the first one to spot the successful trap. In the summer, the windows stayed open; in the winter, they were closed and covered with glass-cloth nailed up with lath. The cold winds rushed through the house and back outside.

When I played inside, I remember that I would line a couple

wood chairs up, one in front of the other. The front of the chairs faced the floor. I climbed on top of the back of one of the chairs so that my legs dangled between the seat of the chair and the rung, just behind the seat of the chair. I sat on the remaining chair brace. This I imagined was my airplane. I leaned forward as the back of the chair leaned toward the floor. I made airplane sounds with bursts of rat-a-tat-tat machine gun sounds. As my chair tipped forward, my plane made deep dives to chase imaginary enemies. I shot down the enemy planes, just as I had seen in the newsreels at the movies in town. I know Mom got a lot of joy out of that commotion.

First Chores

When I got old enough, my mom or sister, who was three years older, washed the dishes and then handed them to me for drying. I dried the dishes and put them on the dinner table. Later, Mom put the dishes away. One day, I was drying dishes and setting them on the table. The table usually sat against the wall in the small kitchen with the drop leaves down. However, on this day the table was against the wall with the drop leaf on the room side positioned outward. I kept drying the dishes and putting the dishes on the drop leaf. But, the narrow table, with the load of dishes on the drop leaf, could not hold the unbalanced weight and suddenly tipped toward me. The table and dishes toppled over with a big crash! I escaped, but the scene was horrific. Broken dishes were everywhere. I waited for the explosion from Mom, but it did not come. Mom pushed the broom and I held the dustpan as we swept up the dishes in silence. My sister smartly vanished to somewhere else in the house.

Another time, I was not so lucky in escaping my mom's wrath. I do not remember the reason for her anger, but I remember her discipline. Whatever I did caused my mom to grab her pink hand mirror. She started spanking me on my butt. I was protesting greatly, and I lifted my heel as she swung the mirror to land a blow. The mirror hit my heel. We both heard the cracking sound; she stopped swinging; I stopped yelling. We both saw that the mirror had cracks across its surface in a number of places. I knew this could not be good. She swung one more time, then cried. For as long as I can remember, she had used that mirror every day. I do not remember any more spankings.

During the school year every morning after the chores, Ken and Barb waited at the road. A small truck stopped. The truck had an enclosed box on the back with a window on each side and a door. Ken and Barb opened the door in the back, climbed into the box on the truck, and were driven away to the Cowles Elementary School (sounds like "coals"). They were returned in the mid-afternoon.

In the winter, it was difficult for the school kids because there was little, if any, heat in the back of the truck. Ken wore long johns with a back trap door, bib overalls, a flannel shirt, four-buckle mud boots, a heavy coat, and a hat. Barb wore a dress, long cotton socks, button and loop mud boots, a heavy coat and, a hat. Being cold was just the way it was.

We kids did not have many clothes. My sister's clothes revealed our poor status and the brand of flour we used. In those days, flour sacks were often patterned so that poor people could use the cloth sacks to sew clothes. We wore the same clothes a number of days in a row. Our new clothes were always a couple sizes too big. When they were finally worn out or too small, they were discarded, used for quilts, or made into rags. Holes were easily mended; a patch of similar material solved the problem. Patches were a part of everyday life and just one more chore.

Laundry was a difficult chore. Mom used the scrub board in a tub of cob-stove heated water. By hand, she wrung out as much water as possible. The washed clothes and bedding were put into a bushel basket and carried to the clothesline outside. Clothespins held the clothes on the wire line. If the day was warm, above 32 degrees, the clothes flapped in the breeze and were usually dry by evening. If the breeze turned to wind, the clothes ended up on the ground or covered with dust. Sometimes we could tell when birds sat on the line because they would leave us presents, and the clothes had to be rewashed. When the air temperature fell below 32 degrees, the clothes froze. The frozen clothes usually fell to the ground like stiff wooden planks. Oftentimes, they also needed to be rewashed. If the frozen clothes were removed from the clothesline before they fell, I helped carry them inside. There they were propped like surfboards around the room to melt into piles, only to be taken back outside in warmer weather to dry.

First Moving Vehicle Wipeout

As I got older, about four, I remember finding an old iron wheel, about twelve inches in diameter that came from a piece of farm equipment. I found a stick that fit into the hole where the axle once went. I learned that if I put one hand on the left side of the stick, and put my right hand on the other end of the stick, I could push the wheel. I looked like a human wheelbarrow. It was a great way to travel! I rolled that wheel everywhere I went. One day, as I traveled along a rough cow path running down the hill through the pasture, the holes that the cows made in the path caused me to wipeout. My speed was too fast for that uneven terrain. The iron wheel bounced up and hit my chin. Unfortunately, my tongue was between my teeth when the wheel made contact. The blood did fly, and I yelled all the way back to my house.

Mom met me at the door and found that I had a scrape on my chin and a gash in my tongue. She wrapped my tongue with a dry cloth, but the bleeding would not stop. The whole family got into the car and traveled down the dirt road with my mom holding that rag around my tongue until we got to Dr. Obert's office. I know one thing; it was hard to yell with Mom holding my tongue out of my mouth with a rag. I thought I was in pain, but when Dr. Obert put that sulfur stick on my tongue to stop the bleeding, I knew a whole new level of pain. Then, the bleeding stopped. Today, when my dentist holds my tongue with dry gauze to examine my mouth, I still think of that day my Mom held my tongue with that dry rag. I gag now, just as I did then.

chapter five
the memories of boyhood

The farm's geographic location determined which school district students would attend. At the time, Cowles was a tiny village of about six square blocks. It had a two-story, brick elementary/high school. My sister and brother both attended the Cowles School District. The school district rules required that when I turned the age of six, I would also attend the Cowles School. The Cowles Elementary School did not have a kindergarten class that I could attend at age five.

Because our school was in Cowles, and because Cowles was as close to our farm as Red Cloud, we often went into Cowles to buy supplies. Gravel roads led to and from the little village. Cowles had several stores lining the gravel main street (Webster Street). I recall the school gymnasium, a general store, a gas station or two, a farm/feed store, tall grain storage bins, and a railroad track running north and south. The Burlington & Missouri River Railroad headed south from Hastings through Cowles to the Amboy rail junction that ran along the Republican River, east to Guide Rock and beyond, and westward to Red Cloud. Small homes were settled in and around the town of Cowles.

One of the best things I remember about Cowles is there was a tall, white, tin-sided garage building. Benches, made from boards and blocks, were put out next to it, and movies were shown on the side of the building after dark. On those rare movie nights, we sometimes got treats from the general store. The movies were the old ones like Laurel and Hardy, Little Rascals, Abbott and Costello, and The Three Stooges. There were newsreels of current or historical events like the war, disasters, and places overseas. As I look back, it seems to me that the Little Rascals may have been my role model for relating to my family and neighbors.

Big Boy Chores

At the age of five, my farm duties solidified. I helped push the hay into the stalls of the barn for the horses and cows. The chickens kept laying eggs, which I had to collect each day with my sister. I did other helpful things as assigned when I tagged along watching my dad and my big brother on weekends and evenings do the chores and tend to the farming.

During harvest, as Mom and Dad handpicked the corn, I started and stopped the two muscular workhorses, Duke and Prince. The wagon was long and narrow. Sideboards (bang boards) were stacked higher on the backside of the wagon so that, as the corn was shucked and thrown into the wagon, the corn landed against the bang board on the backside of the wagon. My parents, and sometimes my brother, walked down the rows of corn. Each person shucked two rows at a time. When the corn hit the bang board, sometimes the corn kernels or ears would glance off it and hit me, the driver of the wagon. When that happened, I complained loudly.

Visiting Grandpa and Grandma Hager

On weekends and Sale Day (Tuesday) when we went to Red Cloud, after selling our farm produce and shopping, we often

stopped at Grandma and Grandpa Hager's house. Their house sat on a hill that sloped down to the back of the house. In the front, there were steps onto a small porch that was covered with vines.

The front door opened into the living room. In the corner of the living room was a fuel oil stove used to heat the house. Grandma had a glass china cabinet full of her treasures. Many times there was a quilt rack with a quilt-in-process along the wall in front of the north window. Oval, gold-framed pictures of old people, who were my great-grandparents, hung on the wall. On the side of the living room were two small bedrooms, just big enough for a bed and a set of drawers. Behind the living room was the kitchen. My grandparents had water in their house. There was a sink in the kitchen and a bathroom in back of the kitchen. Electricity provided plenty of power for lights, a fan, and a radio. Flowered wallpaper and patterned linoleum provided decoration.

On the side of the kitchen was a door that went out onto the roof of the basement porch. Steps led down to the lower level of the yard. There was a large garden, several fruit trees, and a mulberry tree. The full basement was only used for laundry and storage of canned vegetables and fruit. There were old pieces of furniture, boxes, trunks, and other things leftover from a life of farming. The basement was always dark, damp, and musty. Outside the house were several huge cottonwood trees. At the end of the driveway was a garage with Grandpa's 1936 Chevrolet. Despite living in town, a small chicken coop stood next to the garage. A fence held in a dozen or so chickens.

Each day Grandma collected fresh eggs to eat. Also, she let some eggs hatch into little chicks. The chicks became fryers. Grandma made the best fried chicken.

My family rarely ate salad, but Grandma cut lettuce leaves from her garden and soaked the lettuce in sweetened milk. I always thought that was an odd, but tasty, way to eat lettuce. Their garden provided everything for the canned jars in the basement.

If we were at my grandparent's house for breakfast, we always had pancakes with store-bought white Karo syrup—a luxury. I thought white syrup was wonderful! Mom always made our syrup out of brown sugar. I don't know when I first tasted maple syrup.

But, the best food of all was Grandma Hager's special

occasion baked beans. I skipped dessert whenever she made them, so that my stomach could hold second and sometimes third helpings of those baked beans.

Many times my aunts, uncles, and cousins were there. Each family brought potluck dishes. We ate, visited, and played. In the summer, we kids went outside and made cottonwood leaf mats by gathering the green leaves, breaking off the stems, and sewing the leaves together with the stems. Then, we sat on the mats to play games. We watched cars and trucks go by sitting on the front steps near Highway 281.

Sometimes, we snuck into the basement and explored the rooms without our parents knowing about our secret missions. We opened boxes and trunks to see the old hats, dolls, pictures, and clothes. The exploration of the basement was dark, dank, and dangerous.

In the evening when fireflies were out, we gathered them into jars so we could see their lights shine. Before we left for the day, Grandma set out the dessert for one more sugar high.

If we visited in the winter, everyone stayed inside. That was pretty boring.

Grandma Hager spent winters in the kitchen cooking or quilting in the living room. Grandma always wore an apron over her printed, cotton dress. Often she did not wear her false teeth, so when she chewed her food, her chin seemed to touch her nose. She was nice to us kids.

Grandpa Hager spent winters sitting in his overstuffed rocking chair. A standing ashtray stood beside his chair. He always smoked roll-your-own cigarettes; his fingers were stained yellow from the smoke curling up between his fingers.

We kids tried to roll his cigarettes for him. First, we opened the pouch or can of tobacco. Then, we took a single piece of cigarette paper and made a trough in the paper. Next, carefully poured the fragrant tobacco into the trough. Then, we licked one edge of the paper and wrapped the paper around the tobacco. Finally, we licked the paper seam once again and twisted each end closed. Grandpa took the cigarette with a smile on his face and lit it. He inhaled the white, gray smoke with a look of having the best cigarette he ever smoked.

He was fun to tease. He was a very short person. The back of the old rocker was sunken, just like his hump back. He was bald, but he had long, thin, gray hair on one side of his head that he combed over the top of his bald spot. We kids got a kick out of sneaking up behind his chair and mussing up his hair so the long hair stood straight up off the side of his head. He seemed to get a kick out of us kids teasing him. We always got into trouble if we stayed inside too long.

Visiting Grandpa and Grandma Hesman

Grandma and Grandpa Hesman lived on the north end of town. Their house had two unused upstairs bedrooms. It was always chilly in the winter upstairs because there was a door at the base of the stairs that was kept closed. On the stairs hung coats and hats, the steps held boxes, magazines, and other items not worth carrying to the rooms above.

We normally came into the house through the back door and entered the kitchen. There was electricity and water as well at their house. The bathroom was just to the back of the kitchen. To the left of the kitchen was a parlor. There were two downstairs bedrooms: one at the front of the house and one at the back of the house. We never went into those rooms because the doors were always closed. At the front of the house there was a seldom-used living room. Big wood and glass doors separated the parlor and living room.

Grandpa had an oak rocker with a leather seat in the parlor. There was a big oak table and chairs in it also, and along the wall was a long overstuffed couch. Everyone spent most of the time in the kitchen and parlor.

Across the front of the house was a large open porch with a swing that would sit two adults or lots of kids. There were large square tapered pillars holding up the porch roof. From the porch, we could see all the traffic coming and going into Red Cloud on Highway 281.

Outside in the back, and next to the alley, was a garage for Grandpa's gray 1947 Plymouth. There was a grape arbor and a large two-person Klondike chair that Grandpa always sat in to smoke his cigars.

Large elm trees provided plenty of shade to sit under. In front of the grape arbor and his chair, was a large garden. Grandpa and I would sit outside in his big chair watching the birds in the grapevines and the garden growing.

The most interesting memory of Grandma and Grandpa Hesman's house was the large iron heat grate in the center of the parlor room. When the heat was on, I laid on the wood floor and tried to see down into the dark grate. On the edge at the corners, the air was cool and was sucked down into the furnace. In the center of the grate was a large circle out of which came hot air that rushed to the ceiling. From time to time when the heat seemed to subside, Grandpa opened a narrow door in the corner of the parlor and pulled a string that lit a light bulb down in the basement. Then we headed to the basement. I followed him down the narrow wooden steps into the dirt walled, dungeon-like space. At the base of the steps was a pile of black coal lying under a trap door on the outside wall. A large shovel leaned against the earthen wall. In the center of the basement was a large, dirty gray furnace. On the side of the furnace hung a heavy iron door that had peepholes in it to see the flames without opening the door. The large beast of a thing growled in the dimly lit cavern. Grandpa opened the door and threw in several shovelfuls of coal. As he did so, the furnace roared and fiery ash flew out, as if it wanted to grab anyone standing nearby. When Grandpa finished, I was the first one up the steps in an attempt to get out of that scary place. When we got back upstairs, the heat again billowed to the ceiling.

On the wall in the parlor hung a mantel clock chimed to count the hours and chimed once on the half hour. On certain days, Grandpa would take a key and wind the clock in two different places: one place for the time and one place for the chime. The parlor always had a cigar and pipe smell. Grandpa had a spittoon and standing ashtray by his large oak rocking chair. That was my favorite room in the house.

Uncle Fred, Aunt Irene, and my cousins came from Chester, Nebraska sometimes. We had dinners together at Grandma and Grandpa's house. The cousins swung on the porch with glee. We went upstairs and explored the no longer useful things like old magazines, clothes, and broken household items. Back in those days, people kept things because you never knew when you might need a bit or piece of something for a repair or project.

Sometimes the boys and men went fishing at a pond or at the Republican River. Usually, we caught bullheads in the ponds and catfish in the river. They looked the same to me. They both had wide mouths and long whiskers. I always thought they did not look like bulls or cats. When we got back to Grandpa's house, us kids would line up and get our picture taken with the fish.

Victor, Jimmie, Bob, and Ken

Bullheads are hard to clean. They have a sharp horn at the back of their gills and a sharp needle on the fin on their back. If the barb or needle stuck you, the puncture bled profusely and did not heal easily. To clean them, you had to start by cutting off the head. Then, the body was cut open and the guts were pulled out. Next, the fish's skin was peeled down the body away from the flesh. That was the hard part. The adults used pliers for this part by catching the edge of skin at the front of the fish body and pulling the skin away, clear down to the tail. After the fish was skinned, the bodies were floured and fried in a hot iron skillet. The fish fry was the centerpiece of our supper. Mm, mm, good.

Grandpa took all the fish guts, skin, and bones, along with coffee grounds, and buried them in one spot in his backyard. The next time we went fishing, we dug in that spot to collect huge earth worms from the soil. We put them in coffee cans filled with some of the black moist dirt to keep them fresh. As a child, I figured the dirt must be pretty good if the worms liked it so much. So, I went inside and snuck a spoon from Grandma's cabinet drawer. Then, I went out to where the worms grew, took a spoonful of dirt, and ate it. It was not too bad.

One day at my Grandparent Hesman's house, Grandma allowed me to help her churn the cream into butter. The big jar had a rotating paddle inside that rotated when the crank was turned on the top. At first, it was easy to turn the crank. But, as the cream got thicker and thicker, the job of turning the crank got harder and harder. At some point, my grandma had to take over. When the crank could no longer be turned, Grandma took the pale yellow glob out of the jar and put it on a plate. Grandma had a little red ball of coloring that she broke open and poured onto the pale yellow mound of butter. She mixed the coloring into the butter. Soon the butter was bright yellow just like "store-bought butter." Our churned butter on the farm never looked as yellow as my grandma made it. Churning butter with Grandma Hesman is the only memory I have of doing something together with her.

The Funeral

One cold day, our whole family got into the car. It was a sad and quiet ride into town. We arrived at Grandma and Grandpa Hesman's house. Other cars were there too. I recognized some of the people, some I did not. I was told my Grandma Carrie Hesman died. It was December 9, 1947.

A day or so later, dressed in our best clothes, we went into town. At the funeral parlor, there was a small, dimly lit room with lots of flowers and big ribbons with words on them. On the side of the room was a long ornate box with an open lid. Adults were milling around quietly. Any kids who were there were very quiet and wore faces of somber confusion. I remember being lifted up so that I could see inside the ornate box just for a moment. The inside was like a shiny pillow. At first I did not recognize the lady inside. She was pale and white looking. But slowly I saw a reminiscence of her, and I knew it was my grandma. That was the first time I saw a dead person.

In Nebraska, family, friends, and neighbors always helped out by bringing lots of food to the house for after the funeral. As the concerned guests came to share condolences, they ate and talked. My dad needed to go back to the farm and do the chores, so he decided to take the kids with him. His smart plan got us restless kids out of the house where all the adults were visiting.

While Dad did his chores, we kids began making sandwiches. I had a large butcher knife in my hand and was, for some unremembered reason, turning in circles. My cousin Victor stepped into the path of my butcher knife. I don't remember exactly how it happened, but the knife cut right across his nose. Victor's nose lay open like a sliced wiener. We ran out screaming to find Dad. He unhappily took us back to town. Aunt Irene taped Victor's nose back together. Each time Victor and I meet when I am in Nebraska, I cannot look at him without staring at that scar. I smile, and he looks stern. Soon after, we tell each other our own version of how he walked in front of my butcher knife. My version ends with the idea that as he was older than me, he should have known not to step into my knife's path.

The Big Dare

After Grandma Hesman died, we still visited Grandpa Hesman when our family went to town. When we visited his house, he was always sitting on his big chair in the yard; he seemed lonely sitting there. We also saw him downtown at the liquor store where he worked, just up from the Texaco station. Sometimes Grandpa would drive out to the farm to see us.

One day Grandpa Hesman came to the farm in his big '47 Plymouth. For some reason, he came to take us into town. Grandpa Hesman, Mom, my sister Barb, and I were in the car rolling along on the dirt road heading west before we got to Highway 281. Barb and I were in the back seat.

The back doors on the Plymouth opened forward (suicide doors) and there were no seat belts in those days. My sister and I always teased and taunted each other. My sister dared me to open the door. So I did. I pulled on the door handle. The wind caught the car door and flew wide open. With my hand still on the door handle, I was catapulted into the ditch of the road. I was told that Barb said, "Jimmie is gone."

Of course, with the car door wide open, Mom and Grandpa knew for themselves something was definitely wrong. The brakes went on, and the car came to a halt a little ways down the road. I don't remember being picked up or riding home.

The next thing I do remember was being back home with my mom holding me as I protested at the top of my voice. When I was pulled out of the car by the door handle, I landed in the grader ditch, which was full of weeds and sunflowers. I had scratches and abrasions all over. My head was generously scraped, and my hair was pulled loose into bunches and fell onto my shoulders. I was a mess. Mom washed away all the dirt from my scratches and cuts, and then soothed me back to calmness.

As things have turned out, I don't have much hair. My dad and Grandpa Hager were quite bald as well. I like to think, that had I not fallen out of the car onto my head, things might have been different for my hairline.

We Survived the Winter of 1948-1949

When I was five, the snowstorms of 1948-1949 hit Nebraska; seventy to one hundred inches of snow fell that winter. The storms stranded livestock and people all across the farmlands of Nebraska. Our little farm north of town was totally isolated many weeks that winter. After the severe storms, my dad opened the door of our house and dug into the wall of snow that drifted against the house. We kept the shovel inside the house. Deep paths were shoveled between the house, barn, and chicken house.

When possible the driveway was shoveled to the plowed road. After each storm, the melting snow made the creeks high and the mud deep. The deep ruts from cars driving on the muddy roads became frozen overnight. Driving on the country roads was treacherous for farmers trying to get into town to buy or sell their farm products. Hay, feed, and food were dropped from airplanes to farms all across the Midwest that winter. Newspapers, radios, and newsreels at movies documented the winter of 1948-1949.

Our family worked hard to survive that winter.

chapter six
the big move to a new farm

In March of 1949, the landlord sold the farm that my grandparents rented. Consequently, we had to move. My parents decided they would continue to be farmers. In all the snow and ice, we moved our belongings, the remaining livestock, and what little equipment we had to the new farm.

My parents were able to get a government loan to buy the new farm. It was a quarter section of land located eight miles north of Red Cloud and a half-mile west of Highway 281 in Batin Precinct on the south edge of Section 23. The snow and cold were just as bad on the new farm.

The Landscape

The farmhouse and buildings sat on the crown of a hill. A dirt road went by the south side of the farm property. If you looked east, the land dropped down to a creek bed and a bridge. On the far side of the creek was a small hill, and beyond you could see cars, tractors, and trucks traveling on the paved Highway 281. If you listened carefully, you could hear the whine of the mud tires rolling on the pavement as the vehicles traveled north and south. All cars and trucks in the winter and spring needed the aggressive tires, which we called "knobbies," to dig through the mud and snow on the rural dirt roads. The "knobbies" made the tires whine as they got up to speed.

If you looked to the west, you would see another creek bed, a bridge, and a higher hill beyond which you could not see. Our west property line went just beyond the creek to the side of the hill on the west. The property line went north a half-mile. A fence line went east to Highway 281. Another fence ran along Highway 281 back to the road that ran in front of our house. The creeks on both sides of our farmhouse met to the south on the neighboring farm property and together flowed into Crooked Creek which eventually passed around the east edge of Red Cloud and on into the Republican River.

Because of the large snow storms that first winter and spring, the dirt road from the highway to our house was nothing but mud, ice, and snow with ruts six inches deep that clogged the wheels of our '37 Chevy car with mud. When the car could go no more, Dad walked to the farm, started the John Deere tractor that he got for the new farm, and drove the tractor back to where the rest of us were waiting in the cold, stuck car. With the tractor, Dad towed the car to our house. As the snow thawed, the mud and ruts in our yard got deeper and deeper.

The Property

Our new farm had a two-story house, a one-hole privy (outhouse), an underground cellar, a barn, two chicken houses (one large and one small), a small storage shed, a one-car garage right next to a windmill, a car, and a tractor. We still had two workhorses, some cattle, chickens, and pigs. We had a dog to play with and some barn cats to hunt down the mice.  This rural area of the state did not yet have electricity. Lights burned kerosene. Fuel oil was the source of heat. Water came from the windmill pump and was carried to the house about fifty yards away.

A large cottonwood tree provided shade just east of the windmill and cistern. Rows of young evergreen trees ran along our farm yard on the east and west sides for future windbreaks as mandated by the homestead and dust bowl regulations. The house was surrounded with a fence and more evergreen trees. A single olive tree stood in the northwest side of the house yard. Our garden was located not far from the cottonwood tree.

The house was a typical T-shaped farmhouse. It was a two-story house with two bedrooms upstairs; under those rooms on the main level were a living room and bedroom. To the side of the two-story part of the house were a kitchen, a bathroom, and a long enclosed porch.

The kitchen had an icebox and dry sink. There was a cob stove for cooking. The furniture from the old farmhouse fit into the respective rooms of the new house. The living room had a fuel oil heating stove. A little vent in the living room ceiling allowed some heat to reach the two bedrooms upstairs. On the porch was a cream separator and buckets.

The privy was situated outside the fence that surrounded the house. The privy was about eighty feet from the house, which made for a long walk at night in the winter. It had a concrete floor, which covered a large hole in the ground. The concrete floor had a raised box on it with a wooden seat and lid. We used Sears & Roebuck or Montgomery Wards catalogs for toilet paper, which was not too kind on the backside. Some people used corncobs though, which was always worse. The odor and flies were terrible in the summer, and the snow drifted through cracks around the door onto the toilet seat in the winter. It was not a place to spend much time. My business was done quickly and carefully.

Settling In

Our government loan required certain types of crops and livestock. To prevent wind erosion, as had happened during the dust bowl years in Nebraska, we were required to plant a certain number of evergreen trees on the farm, which we did, as you can see in the picture.

The pasture was already fenced so the cattle and horses that we brought that spring from the other farm knew where they belonged. The pigs found a mud hole in back of the barn to make their home. The chickens roamed the farm and went into the chicken coops at night. Dad spent time and money purchasing the right amount of livestock on Sale Days in Red Cloud. Soon there were calves and piglets.

After we moved in, Dad started learning about the farm and where he needed to plant the crops. When the fields could be worked in the spring, Dad spent his time planting the crops: some corn, some wheat, and some other grains that he thought were needed in the fields that were previously planted. The hay fields and pastures remained the same.

My big brother Ken, helped Dad. My sister Barb, helped Mom set up the house. They all did chores every morning and evening: feeding the chickens, milking cows, throwing hay to the cows and horses, and giving slop to the pigs. A supply of corn-cobs was carried from a storage bin to the kitchen for the next day's cooking needs. We did not use wood because there were only a few trees around. After milking the cows in the morning, the milk was run through a hand-cranked cream separator and stored in milk and cream cans.

Jimmie Explores

Blackie the dog and I explored all the buildings and roamed around the property all the way to the creeks.

One day I was exploring under the creek bridge on the west. A small amount of water was running under the bridge. Weeds on both ends of the bridge made the space under the bridge feel like a cave.

As I looked out through the weeds I noticed a green stick crawling up another weed. I moved closer. The moving green stick had big yellow/ brown eyes on the front. The head had long feelers that waved around and a pointed nose. The legs looked like daggers. As I moved closer, the prehistoric looking bug stared right at me.

Suddenly it jumped on me. I could feel its sharp feet and was sure it would bite me. I jumped back, brushing the creature off as I retreated out the other side of the bridge. That was the first time I had been attacked by a stick bug. It took me a while to get up the nerve to go back under that bridge.

Jimmie is Left Hanging

With no electricity, air conditioning in the warmer months came from open windows on the north side of the house in the day and all the windows open at night. Our house was situated so that the only window that was left open during the day was the north window of the house. That window provided light and ventilation into a small room that was used as a bathroom.

With no electricity or water in the house, the bathroom had only a thunder pot for nighttime needs (rather than going outside to the privy), a long galvanized tub, mops, buckets, and brooms. The water, which was carried from the windmill, was heated on the cob stove and mixed with cold water so that it would not scald someone. Only a couple inches of water were used in the washtub.

One spring day it was my turn for a weekly bath. Because I was still too young to do any evening chores, the bath water was prepared. I was instructed to take a bath while the rest of the family did their respective chores. The cool evening air was flowing in through the window of the bathroom as I dipped water all over myself. I decided that I needed to shut the window because the air was making me cold.

Completely naked, I climbed up onto the windowsill and put my hands up on the top edge of the raised lower window. My plan worked in that the window came down. But, what I did not plan was my fingers getting caught. There I was hanging with my fingers stuck between the bottom edge of the upper window and the top edge of the lower window. One finger pinch hurts;

but eight fingers being pinched at once really hurts! I was caught buck naked hanging in the window with no options for self-preservation.

I yelled at the top of my voice. I struggled. And yet, I continued to dangle like a kite caught in a tree. Everyone was in the barn. No one could hear me. No one came to my rescue. Eventually, I gave up and thought someone would find my still, naked body hanging in that window. My fingers had gone numb from the pain.

Finally, Mom finished her chores and returned to a house filled with my screams. She quickly rescued me, wrapped me with a towel, and tried to console me. But it is hard to be consoled when you can see that the person consoling you is having a hard time holding back the laughter. Both my fingers and my pride were severely bruised.

Jimmie Goes to the Hospital

During the winter of 49/50, I started to have throat infections. I often gagged on my food when eating. My voice changed so that I could make sounds like Donald Duck. Everyone got a kick out of my Donald Duck voice.

On one of our trips to town to sell our cream and eggs, my parents took me in to see Dr. Bennett. He decided I needed to get my tonsils out. My blood tests revealed that I needed a series of penicillin shots before I could get my tonsils out. As I took the series of penicillin shots, my butt cheeks, where those shots landed, were itching like crazy. It turned out that I was allergic to penicillin. Dr. Bennett decided that was enough shots and said, "Let's get those tonsils out."

When the big day came for my operation, my parents took me to the Maynard Hospital. I was taken to a room where I undressed and was then covered with a white gown that was open in the back. That little gown failed to cover my itchy butt cheeks. Onto a cold stretcher I went and then was wheeled into a cool room with a big light shining in my face. The nurses lifted me onto another cold surface. I stared up at all these people with masks, staring back at me. Someone told me to take several deep breaths, and a mask was placed over my nose and mouth. I remember clearly thinking, as I breathed deeply, this is not so bad. Then someone dripped some smelly fluid onto the mask. I started to struggle from the horrible smell. I saw blackness with yellow mice running in circles, then a yellow cat started chasing the mice, then I saw a yellow dog chasing.

Maynard Hospital

When I woke up in a hospital bed with my parents standing next to my bed, my throat really hurt. I could hardly swallow. I was given ice cream, which I rarely was fortunate enough to receive. The ice cream felt and tasted good. My mom gave me a toy fire truck from which water could be pumped out of the fire hose. Between the ice cream and the fire truck, I began to feel better. We stayed in the room for a couple hours, I was dressed, and we drove home to the farm.

Jimmie Goes to Church

My Aunt Irene and Uncle Fred started encouraging my parents to go to church. They were Lutherans, so our family joined the Zion Lutheran Church in Red Cloud. The little white church was on the southwest corner of 5th and Chestnut Street. I was baptized on April 22, 1950. Fred and Irene Hesman were my God Parents who stood with me and answered all the questions of the baptism ceremony.

We made many trips into town for church attendance. I went

to Sunday school and Vacation Bible School in the summer at which time I stayed the week with Grandma and Grandpa Hager. I also went to special events like the Christmas skit put on by the kids. I remember that all the children in the Christmas skit got a little bag of unshelled peanuts, ribbon candy, and other hard candy. That was a rare treat in those days.

chapter seven
district 26
the bohemian school

When the summer of 1949 ended, I was six-years-old and ready for school. But there was a problem. At School District 26, students were required to take kindergarten before they could start first grade. Kindergartners started when they were five.

But I was already six! The only option was to be a six-year-old kindergartner.

Miss Bliss was my first teacher. My brother and sister went to the same one room school. Barb started at this new school as a fifth grader and Ken started as a sixth grader. The school was located a half-mile west and a half mile south from our house.

The District 26 School was called the Bohemian School because the Webster County Batin Precinct had a large number of Czechoslovakian families farming in the area.

The One-Room Schoolhouse

The schoolhouse was a one-room school with a closed-in porch for coats and boots. The one room had windows on the north and south sides. The back wall had blackboards on each side of a big pot-bellied stove and wood box. Penmanship letters were lined across the room above the blackboards. Eight different grade level books were in bookshelves lined up under the windows.

Wood desks with a folding bench in front were lined up into four or five rows facing the back wall. The smallest desks were near the teacher's desk. The desktops had deep marks carved in the edges from past students wanting to leave their mark. The teacher's desk was off to the side toward the back wall of the classroom.

Between one of the windows on the sidewall was a picture of George Washington with his white hair, which I eventually found out was a wig. On the wall toward the front of the school was a United States flag. The walls were yellowish white and the floors were dark brown, long boards running the length of the room. Other school supplies were here and there on shelves.

There were no lights; only kerosene lamps were used. Lighting was not a problem usually because school was always held during the day. Although on stormy days the light coming through the windows was dim.

The older kids pumped water from a pump near the school and put the water into a big crock water jar. The crock had a heavy lid, large blue rings around the outside, a push button valve to let the water out, and a tin dipping cup hanging on the side. We all shared that dipping cup.

The most intriguing item to me was a device that had a large golden ball, the sun, on a pedestal with an arm that rotated around the big ball. On the arm was another blue and green ball, the earth, which had a small yellow ball, the moon, which quickly rotated around the blue and green ball as arm was rotated around the golden ball. Chains on sprockets hung below the arm to make everything work together. I came to realize that device demonstrated how our earth rotated around the sun and how the moon rotated around the earth.

The school was located on the west side of the gravel road in the midpoint of the section of land. All around the schoolyard were fields that sometimes had wheat, sometimes corn, or whatever the farmer, who owned the property around the school, decided should be rotated for the health of the soil. In back of the school building was a woodshed. Farther out was a privy. To the south side was a swing and merry-go-round. Beyond was an open, grassed playground. In all, the school set on about an acre of land.

Before School Buses

Getting to school was a chore. We went on foot or on a bicycle through the rain, snow, or shine. A few lucky kids were brought or picked up by their parents. There was no school bus. The road west from our house was dirt for a half-mile, and the road south was gravel. The three of us kids started out walking together, but my legs were shorter so my brother Ken ended up walking way ahead. My sister Barb often hung back with me until we got to the corner where we turned south. Sometimes we met up with the neighbor kids coming from the north. The smaller kids always lagged behind. Eventually, we all ended up at the school.

When it came to riding bicycles, I could not ride one, nor did I have one. One day a bike appeared. My parents said it was mine. It was a full sized bike with no fenders. The beat-up bike had no chain guard. It was a bare bones bike. My dad adjusted the seat as low as it would go and put a basket on the front for my lunch bucket and books. It was my first bike, and I liked it. This two-wheeled machine opened up a whole new world of freedom for me.

My feet did not touch the ground. When I rode the bike, I held onto the handlebars and slid across the middle bar from side to side. To start, I had to find a post or tree, get on the bike, and push away for a good start. Later I learned to get a running start and swing my leg over the seat. When I wanted to stop, I would brake; then, just before falling over, I would jump off. Stopping was a dangerous task.

When the roads were dry, we rode our bikes to school. I could keep up with my sister and brother, until we got to the hill. I had to push my bike to the top before I could get back on and ride to the next hill. Sometimes my sister waited for me at the top of each hill.

I always had holes in my right pant leg. Remember, no chain guard. As I slid back and forth across the middle bar, my pant leg often got caught in the chain sprocket. That was a major problem since my feet did not touch the ground. If I was going up hill, I quickly stopped and fell over. But I was then pinned with one leg under the bike and the other caught on the upper side in the chain and sprocket. Sometimes someone would be there to help, other times I had to pull until my pants tore out of the chain and sprocket. If I was traveling down a hill and caught my pants, I would coast faster and faster because I could not brake. If I was lucky enough to make it to the bottom and up a little ways on the next hill, I stopped by falling over as described above. If I hit ruts or gravel while going downhill with my pant leg caught, it ended in a disastrous crash with me unwillingly attached to the bike. When I recovered and got free, sometimes the chain was off, so I had to thread it back on or push the bike the rest of the way to school or home. Despite the crashes I remained in one piece with only scrapes and bruises. All in all, I made it to and from school with greater and greater efficiency.

In rain or snow, all of us kids just slogged through the mud and snow. We were wet and cold when we got to school. All our coats, hats, gloves, and socks were placed near the pot-bellied stove to dry out before we made our way home.

Some winters the roads were drifted so high with snow that no vehicles could get through. The first roads to be plowed were the mail and school routes. Our one-mile dirt road in front of our house was one of the last to be plowed; consequently, the first half-mile to school was always the hardest. If the ponds were frozen, we crossed the fence near the mailbox corner and slid on the iced-over pond in a pasture just for fun.

Bicycles with Icicles

I remember one cold day, while at school, there was a freezing rain. When we got out of school, we all left on our bicycles to head to our homes. When we got to the corner where our mailbox was located, my brother, sister, and I turned east onto the dirt road toward home. The hill was rutty from the frozen car tracks. I generally had to push my bike to the top of the first hill. My brother and sister went on ahead.

As I pushed my bike, I noticed icicles hanging on the handlebars of my bike. The icicles looked inviting, so I reached out with my tongue and licked the icicle. My tongue froze onto the handlebars. That was bad!

I had to walk my bike up the hill, down the other side, and up the hill into our yard. On that rutty road, I learned how long a tongue could be as my bike bounced around and pulled painfully on my tongue.

When I got to the house, I yelled as loud as I could with my tongue still frozen to the bike. Mom looked out and saw my predicament. She rescued me by pouring warm water onto the metal bar and my tongue.

What a relief to be free, but I did lose some tongue skin out of the ordeal. My family cut me no slack that evening as they laughed about my first lesson on not putting a wet tongue on a frozen piece of metal.

School Time

Going to a one-room school with a dozen children in any of the nine grades, Kindergarten through eighth, was a challenge for us kids. I am sure it was a challenge for the teacher as well. The teacher had to work with eighth graders, while giving attention to a kindergartener or first grader. That meant there needed to be lesson plans for all subjects with variations for each grade and student as they progressed. I am sure the very young students were such a distraction that the seventh and eighth graders were short changed. As I recall though, we were proud of our school and teacher. The students were helpful to each other and learned how to help teach the younger kids.

The school always seemed to be hot or cold. In the winter, the kids pushed the desks and chairs up as near as possible to the pot-bellied stove. The older kids kept the fire in the stove stoked. In hot weather we opened windows and doors.

Recess Games

I remember the recesses and lunch hours most of all. We played many group games. In the spring and fall we played softball. Once in a while, another country school came to our school to play a game of softball. The Tin School House, which was located about ten miles north of Red Cloud right along Highway 281, was one school that we played. The day of a softball game was as exciting as it could get for a kid.

Another game was Andy-Andy Over. One team threw the ball over the roof of the school building while calling out "Andy-Andy Over." The other team tried to catch the ball before it hit the ground. The throwing team tried to throw the ball in different locations to make it hard for the other team to anticipate where the ball would come over. If the receiving team caught the ball, they would run around the school building. The person with the ball tried to tag as many kids as possible by hitting them with the ball as they ran to the other side of the school. If you were tagged, you joined the other team. If the receiving team did not catch the ball, they threw it back over shouting "Andy-Andy Over." The big kids threw the ball, but everyone went for the ball when it needed to be caught. When all the team members were captured to one team, the game was over.

Pump-Pump Pull Away was a running game we played where two sides lined up at opposite ends of the playground. Someone in the middle pulled a student from behind the line onto the field. Then everyone tried to run to the other side of the field without being caught. Those caught joined those in the middle. Of course, soon there were more people in the middle, making it harder for those who had to cross the field. The last person caught trying to get to the other side was the winner.

We spent a lot of time riding our bikes near the school during recess as well. We created paths off the road into the grader ditch and up the bank to the higher landing. Then we went back down to the road on a different path. The higher we could jump with the bike, the better. Sometimes we crashed, but that was part of the fun. We were tough on our bikes.

In the winter, when the weather was clear, we played Fox and Geese. In this game, a large pie-shaped set of paths was created in the snow. We made an outer circle with spokes going into the middle. Someone was chosen to be the fox. All the other kids were geese. The fox chased the rest of the geese, using the paths that were created in the snow. Those being chased could not go out of the paths. When you were caught, or if you left the paths, you had to leave the game. The last person to be caught won the round.

Many times good, old-fashioned, winter snowball fights broke out. During winter recess, we got cold and wet again. So, inside we went back to the pot-bellied stove to strip off our coats, hats, boots, and socks in the hopes that they were dry by the time we put them on again to walk home. On heavy winter days we stayed inside. We colored, and played group games or board games. It was always boring to me when we stayed inside.

Chores at School

Everyone had school chores as well. At the end of the day, the older kids helped clean the school by sweeping the floors, cleaning the chalk off the blackboards, emptying the trash for the burn-barrel, and bringing in a new supply of wood or corncobs inside for the stove the next day.

The smaller students put new chalk on the blackboard rail. We also helped clean the erasers by taking them outside and banging them together with our hands to knock the chalk out of the erasers. Then the erasers were brought back in and evenly distributed onto the blackboard rail.

All the students straightened the desk rows and put their own items away in their desk.

The Burn-barrel Chore

One fall day, it was my turn to gather the trash and take it out to be burned. Another student and I started the fire in the burn-barrel. It was a breezy fall day, and the grass was dry. A breeze blew some of the burning paper out of the barrel and onto the grass. The dry grass caught on fire. We both started stomping the fire out. Soon there were several small grass fires spreading in the field. So we stomped faster. After a few more minutes, we realized we were in trouble. We ran back into the schoolhouse and told the teacher the field was on fire. Everyone ran to stomp out the fires. We had no water.

Our teacher dialed central (the main telephone operator in Red Cloud) on the crank telephone. Our teacher reported the fires and asked for the fire department to be called out. With the old crank phones, there was one ring that everyone was allowed to pick up and listen to the caller and the receiver. That ring was like a public alarm system. You could hear the other private party rings made for the other callers on the line, but you were not supposed to listen in on those calls (but people did anyway).

In no time at all, the farmer nearest the school came and took charge of the situation. Obviously he had picked up the call when he heard our teacher make her emergency call to central. Between the students and the farmer, the fire was under control by the time the volunteer firemen and fire truck made it seven-and-a-half miles out from Red Cloud.

The parents also began to arrive at the school to help and insure that their children were safe. All the kids enjoyed seeing the fire truck in action and the excitement of an uncharacteristic school day.

My schoolmate and I did not get in trouble for the fire because everyone was happy that no one was hurt and that the school did not burn down. Our school building was the second District 26 School building; the first one did burn down.

District 26 Christmas Pageant

Around Christmastime, the big kids started stringing wire across the width of the schoolroom near the front wall. Then they strung two wires from the wall to the other wire. Black cloth was hung on hooks from the wire so that the cloth made two side rooms and a larger room in the middle. This configuration made a stage area and a dressing room on each side. We practiced for a Christmas play. We made paper figures, like stars and evergreen trees, to hang on the cloth walls for a Christmas scene.

One late afternoon before Christmas, all the parents came to the school. The full schoolroom was kept cozy by the hot pot-bellied stove. We students put on our Christmas play for our parents. We sang Christmas songs and put on skits about the Christmas season. It was scary being in front of all the parents and performing our parts. Afterward we had refreshments.

Parting Thoughts

It seemed that each year we had different teachers. They got married or went on to finish their college education. As a new teacher took on the new school year, the school curriculum changed to meet the needs of the grade levels and the number of students for that year. The eighth graders left, and new little kindergarteners came in.

My brother graduated from District 26 after his eighth grade year; he went back to the Cowles School District the fall of 1952 as a freshman. My sister and I continued on at District 26 until we eventually moved into Red Cloud in January of 1954.

chapter eight
the rural farming lifestyle

One thing about farming in the 1950s—it was risky business. The small farms, like my parents had, could only produce enough grain, hay, dairy, produce, and livestock, if everything went just right, to generate enough revenue to pay the monthly loan payments to the banker. Farmers Home Administration Act of 1946 (FHA) backed loans by the government required certain farming improvements that dictated various planting requirements and erosion prevention methods that were costly and time consuming. Horse farming was no longer cost effective so tractors and machinery were needed to keep up with the changing farming methods. Fertilizers, seed, and fuel for the tractors and heating oil for our house were very expensive. We had no electricity so every activity was labor intensive. A successful growing season was as elusive as predicting the weather; the Great Plains got it all: hail, tornadoes, drought, floods, blizzards and wind.

Every family was pretty much on their own. When sickness, accidents, or disasters happened, the neighbors were always helpful as they could be. Most farmers had no life insurance or health insurance. It was only when the pain or sickness was so great that they were forced to consider going to a doctor or get medicine. Much of the time, merchants and doctors provided short term credit so farmers could balance their bills with the revenue from their farm. The farming parents were driven to make ends meet. The farmer's kids were part of the required helping hands needed to get all the work done.

The seven-day work week started at daylight and ended at dusk. The seasons dictated the nature of work on the farm: preparing the soil, planting the seed, fertilizing, weeding, harvesting grain, caring for newborn livestock, feeding the livestock, milking the cows, selling or butchering the livestock, fixing machinery for the next planting season, and repairing fences to keep the livestock in their proper place. Of course, there was cleaning manure from the barn and chicken houses, and in the winter clearing snow between the house, windmill, and all the buildings, doing all the household chores, and for kids doing their school homework.

For our family, spending money was sparse, but food was always on the table because we spent our days raising and growing most of our food there on the farm. What we did not eat we sold. Trips to town were highlights of each week. Selling the week's produce, eggs, and cream in exchange for the different kinds of food, spices, clothes, and household items that the farm could not provide allowed us to have more diverse items at home.

Farming was a risky business, but farming was the life our young family chose.

Spring Planting

When signs of spring started to appear, my dad began to get all the farm equipment ready for the season. My brother was now old enough to drive a tractor so we needed to get another one. He got an old red, crank style Farmall tractor.

Starting these tractors was not easy. The John Deere started by turning a big flywheel on the side of the tractor. When it ran, the sound was a pup-pup-pup sound. When the John Deere worked hard, the pup-pup sound became slower and huskier. The Farmall had a crank on the front end just above the narrow front wheels. My dad would grab the crank and give it a strong, quick turn clockwise. When the engine began to fire, the crank kicked forward enough that the engine could keep turning, but the crank stayed still, hanging down just above the front wheels. However, if the engine backfired, watch out! The crank would suddenly thrust counter clockwise for a short and dangerous moment. A person's hand or arm could be broken in an instant. Dad always started the tractors himself in the morning so they could warm up before working.

After the morning chores, Dad took off into one of the fields.

All the fields needed to be plowed to break the soil and turn it over. The plowed ground with its large chunks of dirt was sliced into smaller pieces of soil using a disc. Next, the ground was harrowed to spread and level the dirt into a nice smooth and flat soil ready for planting. Finally, the lister was used to plant each of the grains of seed at just the right depth for the seeds to grow into rows of corn.

If wheat was being planted, all the soil preparation of plowing and harrowing took place. But in the final step for planting wheat, a wide machine called a drill dug small furrows into which grains of wheat were dropped and the soil was pushed back over the seeds. Within a week, the seeds germinated. Tender tufts of green wheat pushed up out of the soil.

My brother helped Dad with the preparations of the fields after school and on weekends. One thing is for sure: a farmer always knew every square inch of his farmland after having to work the land so many times before plants broke through the ground. Oh yes, after each day on the tractor, the evening chores still needed to be done.

In early spring of 1950, there was a problem with the planting season. Dad prepared the fields for planting, but he became sick with a lung infection before the seeds could be planted. My parents did not know how they could continue farming if the crops were not planted at the right time. One morning, tractors could be seen coming down our road

with listers attached to each tractor. The farmers all pulled into our farm and prepared their equipment for planting. I had never seen so many farmers with their tractors ready for planting in one place. The farmer's wives came that day and prepared dinner (in

Nebraska, the noon hour meal is called dinner; the evening meal is called supper) for the visiting farmers. By sundown, all the seeds had been planted in the appropriate fields. The farmers and their tractors traveled home that evening. My parents were so very thankful for our good neighbors.

As the spring progressed, the bare fields started to look green. Little plants lined up in never-ending rows. They were tiny, then several inches tall; by the time we got out of school in May, the fields were well underway to being large fields of rows and rows of lush green plants a foot or so high. Now, the breeze blowing across the rolling hills could be seen as the tops of the plants moved back and forth.

Because we did not have irrigation, we needed a gentle rain from time to time to provide water for the crops. If the rain and wind came as a storm, it could knock down the new plants and stunt their growth. If hail came in a storm, the crops were shredded. The fields would then need to be replanted, but only if there was enough growing season left for the plants to mature before harvest. My parents were thankful for rain, but always talked about the possibility of a storm.

Making Hay

Another crop we grew was alfalfa. It's a nutritious type of hay used to feed the cattle. As the alfalfa fields began to green up and grow about a foot high, the work turned to tending to the first cutting of hay.

First, the green alfalfa was mowed down using a sickle mower pulled behind the tractor. The mower had a long, flat arm that was dropped down level with the ground. The sharp sickle blade consisted of a flat bar with triangular blades riveted to the bar. The sickle blade slid back and forth behind pointed horns that stuck out in front of the long arm. As the arm was pulled through the alfalfa, the sharp sickle mowed down the alfalfa plants.

The cut alfalfa was becoming hay. After cutting, it was left to dry on the ground. When it was almost dry, we raked it. We used a tine rake that had two large iron wheels about ten feet apart. In between the wheels on a frame were many "u" shaped steel rods called tines. They were turned so the points of the tines dragged on the ground. The many tines created a big rake. High on top and in the middle of the rake was an iron seat and a long locking handle. A rider, like my brother, sat high on the seat and rode on the rake as the tractor pulled it. When the tines were down on the ground, the hay was raked into the round rake tines. Every so many yards, the long handle was pushed forward. The tines were lifted, and the hay rolled out of the rake. Immediately the long handle was pulled back into its locked position to rake another pile of hay. As this process occurred time after time, long rows of rolled up hay began to emerge across the field. It was like magic to watch my brother ride that rake with my dad on the tractor creating such a site across the rolling hills. I wished that I could be sitting high on that rake seat pushing that handle to make those rows. But I was too small. So after a while my dog Blackie and I would go off to do other things.

In a few days, assuming there was no rain to make the hay wet, the rows of hay would be dry enough to gather it onto hayracks (a large wagon with open wooden side rails). This is where the whole family got involved. Sometimes my uncle and cousins joined in, and then we would help them do their hay on their farm.

The small kids got into the hayrack. A rope net was carefully laid out across the bottom of the hayrack. The ends of the rope net hung out on the front and back. One of the older kids drove the tractor that pulled the hayrack along side the rows of hay. The adult men used pitchforks and pitched the dry hay out of the rows up into the hayrack. The kids jumped on the hay as it was pitched into the hayrack. Our jumping around tamped the loose hay so that it became compacted, and more hay could be thrown onto the load. Halfway through the load, another rope net would be laid out across the wagon of hay. And more hay was pitched on top.

When the hay was piled high on the hayrack, we kids rode on top of the full hayrack back to the livestock barn. The hayrack heaved forward and backward and rocked side to side as the tractor pulled the load. This motion resulted in a scary and exciting ride as we traveled on the farm path back to the barn.

When we got to the barn, the smaller kids jumped off the large load, headed into the barn, and climbed up into the hayloft where the action was about to happen. The tall barn had a roof peak that reached well beyond the end of the barn. A huge barn door was dropped open to the side of the barn. Across the peak of the barn to the outside was a steel rail track. On the rail was a trolley device with a long rope connected to it that reached the hayloft floor. Another rope ran from the drawbar of the tractor, through a pulley on the rolling trolley device and down to the hayrack parked outside under the peak of the barn. The rope was hooked to the ends of the rope net under the hay on the hayrack.

When the tractor was carefully driven forward, the rope net tightened around the hay and up it went. The giant bundle of hay rose to the peak of the barn, and suddenly the track device raced along the overhead track into the barn. From inside the barn, the giant bundle of hay entering the open door of the barn looked like an enormous monster invading the darkness of the hayloft. The screeching track rollers carried the load overhead along the top of the barn; at the right time to fill the space in the hayloft, my dad pulled the trip rope reaching up to the track device.

All at once, the giant load dropped out as the rope net released its heavy load. Down into the hay loft the hay came, hitting its mark most of the time. When the load hit the loft floor, the barn creaked as it strained to take the weight. The whole hayloft room filled with rushing air and dust.

The trolley was pulled back to the outside peak for the second rope net full of hay to be delivered to the hayloft in the top of the barn. When the air cleared, we kids scrambled down the loft ladder out of the barn and back onto the hayrack to head out and gather another load. This process continued until enough hay had been hauled into the barn. As the summer went on, the alfalfa was cut two or hopefully three times. When the barn was full, the hay was hauled near the pastures and stacked into large haystacks for the livestock to eat later in the winter.

In the fall when our relatives came to our farm for a visit, we kids went out to the haystacks in the late evenings. We climbed high onto their tops, made nests, and looked into the early evening sky. As the sky darkened, we could see all the millions of stars. Some stars twinkled and some did not. Some were bright and some could hardly be seen. We watched the shooting stars streak across the black sky. The Milky Way was seen off in the far distances of the universe. We looked for the man in the moon; sometimes the moon was a golden harvest moon; sometimes it was only a sliver or not even in the sky. Clouds traveled in front of the moon to give it a mysterious look. I learned where to find the Big Dipper, the North Star, and the Small Dipper. When it was time for the company to leave for their homes, we slid off the haystacks and ran back to the house.

Horsing Around

We had horses on the farm. A couple horses were large workhorses named Duke and Prince; another was my brother's riding horse, named Queeny. The other horse, Trixie, was a Pinto pony that belonged to my sister Barb. Trixie was given to Barb by my Cousin Waunie Lee's parents. They lived in Superior, Nebraska and had no place to keep a horse. Our farm was a good place for Trixie to live. Trixie was white with large brown spots. On weekends, Aunt Frances and Uncle Art came with Waunie Lee in tow to visit us and ride the "pony." All of the kids took turns riding Trixie, sometimes three or more kids rode at a time. We had great fun playing and riding the horses. Sometimes when too many kids got on Trixie's back, she would suddenly stop and lower her head. All of the riders would slide down her neck into a pile of youthful humanity. We got up, laughing, and pushing to see who could climb back onto that pony first.

One Saturday, Barb and I went to get the mail. She rode Trixie. I rode my bike. Off we went a half-mile on the country road over the hill and down to the mailbox. We got the mail and started to return home. The road from the mailbox was uphill.

Barb was strong enough that she could ride the bike up the hill. We agreed that I could ride Trixie. Trixie was a fairly large horse, and I was a fairly small boy. Going up the hill went well. When we crested the top of the hill, Barb was able to pick up speed and travel quite fast down the other side of the hill on the bicycle.

When Trixie saw Barb and the bike going down the hill fast out of the corner of her eye, she set out down the hill on a dead run. I was on top of her with only a bridle. My legs were too short to keep me on her back by pushing my knees into her sides. As she raced Barb on the bike down the hill, I began to lose my hold. I began to slide down and under Trixie's neck. My arms and legs were wrapped around her tight but now I was hanging on under her head for dear life. I was yelling for Trixie to stop, but she refused to let the bicycle win her race.

Fortunately, my dad was working the field near the road just west of the house. He saw that the horse's rider was hanging under the neck of the horse. He stopped his tractor and went to the center of the road. As Trixie continued her run, and as my grip on her neck was beginning to loosen, Dad was able to stop her by grabbing the bridle. I fell off onto the ground. I was shaking and furious. I did not understand why my sister and Trixie did not stop.

A Sticky Situation

One of the exciting things that happened in our farmhouse was that through the spring and summer we started noticing honeybees on the sticky fly tape hanging in our kitchen. And we could hear the buzzing of a beehive on the outside wall of our kitchen. One day I felt a sudden burning on the underside of one of my toes. A bee had stung me. I think that was the first time I received a bee sting. Finally, my parents decided it was time for something to be done about those bees.

A man came to our house. He had a beehive box and a smoke can that he used to blow smoke into the wall of our house. Then he and my dad took the siding boards off the house. Inside the cavities of the wall were thousands of bees and mounds of honeycombs hanging on the studs of the wall. The beekeeper gathered the bees into his hive. My dad cut the honeycombs out of the wall. The bees went with the beekeeper and my parents processed the honey and canned the honey into jars. We stored the honey in the cellar. Dad repaired the hole in the wall. I don't remember that the bees ever returned. But we appreciated that sweet, sticky honey!

The Storm Cellar

Right next to the house on the north side, we had a storm cellar that provided protection for our family during dangerous weather. It was also a place to store canned food and produce from the garden.

The storm cellar entrance was out in the grass. It had a wooden door with stairs that went down into the dark, damp underground room.

Inside, there were bugs, spiders, and sometimes snakes hanging out. The cellar walls were lined with wooden shelves filled with cans of honey, fruit, and meat, giving the appearance of an underground grocery store. Right in the middle of the ceiling of the cellar was a pipe that went through the concrete ceiling and the dirt on top of the roof outside the cellar. That chimney let in a little light and allowed fresh air to circulate in the cellar.

When Mom and us kids first checked out the cellar after we moved to the farm, we found a tin can that was heavy. If we shook it, it sounded like something was inside. We pried the lid off. It was full of rolled up money and lots of coins. We thought we had struck it rich. When we examined the money, we could see that it was a foreign currency. It was German marks and German coins. That was interesting to us kids since it had not been long after the end of World War II against Nazi Germany. The money was not worth anything except to bring out for play from time to time. We kids would count the money, examine the coins, and wonder about the person who had originally owned the money. We wondered how German money got into our cellar.

Tornadoes!

Nebraska is part of Tornado Alley. Every spring and summer we read newspaper stories of tornadoes striking various parts of the Midwest: Nebraska, Kansas, Missouri, and other nearby states. Towns were completely destroyed. Many deaths and injuries were described in the newspapers from the rural towns. I remember in spring of 1953 we heard about the tornado that literally destroyed Hebron, Nebraska. Hebron was just north of Chester where Uncle Fred and Aunt Irene lived. We got in the '37 Chevy and drove to Red Cloud. When we hit Highway 136, we turned east. Highway 136 took us right into Hebron. We drove right up the main street of Hebron. As I looked out the windows of our car, I saw utter devastation. Houses were split in two, turned over, piled into wood splinters and crushed bricks, or they were completely gone. Cars and trucks were turned over and thrown against buildings. The main street buildings were caved in. There were no roofs or they were completely flattened to the ground.

People were busy trying to clean up and salvage what they could. As we drove through the town we remained quiet, overwhelmed by the scene. When we hit Highway 81, we turned south to go on into Chester. Chester was not hit by the tornado.

The Storm

Many times the skies darkened with storms that traveled across our farm. One evening the sky turned very black with lower white clouds moving around.

The air became still and eerie. As I watched the sky, the underside of the heavy black clouds dropped down with pointed cloud funnels. They were rising up and falling down from the bottom of the black cloud. It was as if I was watching the underside of the earth and worms were poking their heads out and hanging down. I knew we were in for a tornado.

My family ran from the barn; all of us quickly dropped down into the cellar. My dad struggled to pull the door closed. As we waited, my dad opened the cellar door so we could peek outside. The light in the sky was a greenish yellow.

A loud thunderous noise startled us from outside as Dad locked the cellar door tight. Suddenly, the rain and wind started tearing at the locked cellar door. It was like having a wild beast growling and gnashing at the protective cellar door. We all cowered down in the cellar amongst the shelves of food imagining what was happening outside to our crops and home. Hail pounded on the cellar door like an angry drummer. We could hear wood being torn apart. I was terrified. Then the hail just stopped. The heavy rain turned to mild rain and then nothing. Just the silence remained after the spent storm had come and gone.

As Dad unlocked the cellar and slowly opened it, the light outside was turning to sunshine. The storm had indeed passed.

Streams of water and mud ran away from our yard, down the ruts in the road, filling the ditches and creeks nearby. Thankfully, all of our buildings stood but one—our largest chicken house had flipped upside down onto its roof. The chickens that survived the horrendous wind and hail looked awkward and dazed by the experience. We gathered the remaining chickens into the other chicken coop. That evening the storm was all we could talk about. We were thankful that all of us along with our home, livestock, and crops survived. We were thankful our tornado was not as destructive as the one that had hit Hebron.

Chicken Tending

The chickens were important to our family. Not only did we sell eggs in town, but also they were an important source of food for our family. We ate the eggs, and we ate the chickens. My sister Barb was older, so she had more responsibilities to care for the chickens. I was her helper.

I fed the chickens cracked corn. I also carried water from the pump to put into their watering containers. We bought sacks of tiny shells to add to the chicken feed, which made the eggshells stronger. We put fresh hay in the nests from time to time.

Once or twice a day my sister and I went into the chicken house to gather the eggs. We were very quiet so that we did not startle the chickens. The hens rested on their nests quietly clucking. We reached in under each hen. Sometimes the hen would peck our hands and arms as we reached in under her. It was always nice and warm under the hen. We felt around in the bottom of the nest and slowly took the eggs we found from the nest carefully putting them into a bucket. After we gathered all the eggs, if it was morning, we opened the chicken house trap door so the chickens could go outside. In the evening, we closed the little trap door so that predator animals like foxes, coyotes, and badgers could not get to the chickens.

We never made friends with the chickens because eventually they were destined to be dinner. When it was time to eat one, Mom picked out a chicken that was just right for the meal. To catch a chicken we used a long wire with a hook that went around the chicken's leg. When the chicken, which was the loser for the day, was chosen, the wire hook was quickly thrust under the chicken followed by a sudden pull to tighten the trap. This resulted in an angry chicken being snared.

Soon, the chicken met its end at the chopping block. Its entrails were removed. We saved the gizzard, heart, and liver for eating. I always ate the heart. The chicken body was dropped into hot boiling water for a minute or so. The boiling water made it easier to pull all the chicken feathers from the chicken. The naked chicken was cut for frying or left whole for roasting.

That is not the entire chicken story. Because we did not have good equipment for incubation of the eggs, most of the time we brought home some little chicks purchased at the feed store. The little yellow fuzz balls on legs were kept in a box with a light that made enough heat to keep them warm. When we looked in their box, they cheeped at us for their food and water. Some died, but most grew into young chickens to be egg layers or fryers. I always thought it was better to be chosen as an egg layer. There were always several roosters to tend to the hens and wake the farmyard up each morning.

As expected, nothing went to waste on a farm. Once or twice a year we covered our faces with handkerchiefs and went into the chicken house with shovels. The dirt floors were covered with chicken poop. Not only did the chickens need a clean chicken house to prevent diseases, the chicken manure made excellent fertilizer for the garden. It was a dirty job. I liked to tell adults that sometimes I lost and found my gum three times when I cleaned out the chicken house. It was a bad joke.

chapter nine
trips to town

Once or twice a week, our family went to town. In the summer, we went on Tuesdays because that was Sale Day. Sale Day was when the auction barn auctioned off livestock. Sometimes we stopped at either or both of our grandparents' houses. Other times, we spent the whole day downtown.

Hanging Out Around Main Street

We took the cream can to the IGA grocery store. The eggs were dropped off at Archer Produce and Feeds. Mom shopped for our other groceries. Sometimes Mom went to JC Penney's or the Ben Franklin 5 & 10. I liked the 5 & 10 store because they had a lot of toys that I wished could be mine. My dad went to the livestock auction to see if he should buy cows or hogs. Also, he went to the North Pool Hall to play pool and drink some beer.

To kill time while we waited for Dad, Mom and I went to the city park at the end of Webster Street, the main street in town. The park was always fun because there were long swings that swung me up really high. There were teeter-totters and merry-go-rounds. There were benches in the shade of the tall elm trees. There was, and still is, a large,

City park drinking fountain

brass bell mounted on a concrete foundation that I always spent some time climbing on and around. I played on the band platform by jumping off the sides to the ground. A drinking fountain right in the middle of the park flowed continuously with water, so I could drink all I wanted. This was a treat for a kid who carried water from the windmill to the house for a drink of water.

Sometimes we got to go to the movies. That was really a treat. To get popcorn was out of this world. We saw newsreels of war, weather, and pictures of faraway places. Cartoons were a favorite: *Tom and Jerry*, *Bugs Bunny*, *Goofy*, and *Donald Duck* to name a few. Then came the feature movie: cowboy shows, comedy shows, and music and dance shows.

Sometimes when Mom was shopping for groceries at the IGA, she let me go next door to the John Deere tractor store. There amongst the big tractors was a riding John Deere tractor. I rode the small pedal tractor around and under the big tractors. When the maintenance garage door was open on Saturdays, I could even circle into the garage between all the other tractors in the shop. Riding that pedal tractor on the smooth floors around that store was the highlight of my visits to town. If we were lucky, the Tom's Candy truck was parked outside the grocery store delivering a supply of candy. When kids ambushed the driver of the candy truck at the store, he seemed to enjoy giving us kids a couple pieces of candy for free as a treat.

Hanging Out at the Pool Hall

Sometimes I was allowed to go into the pool hall where my dad was visiting his buddies. I sat on the high wrought iron chairs lined along the outer walls and watched the games being played. The tall chairs made it easy to see the balls being hit on the surface of the pool table. The North Pool Hall had a long tall bar where men sat to drink beer, smoke, and play dice using a leather cup from which they threw the dice. Spittoons were scattered amongst the tall stools. A big mirror framed the back of the bar; stacks of cigarettes, cigars, and tobacco cans were displayed for sale. An assortment of pipes and cigarette holders were laying around.

Tall cardboard displays held various assortments of Zippo lighters: the lighter that the wind could not blow out. My dad had a Zippo lighter. He could be driving his tractor and with one hand, open the lighter lid, stroke the flint wheel, hold the fire from the lighter to his cigarette, and light his cigarette. It became red hot as he drew the smoke into his lungs all while facing into the Nebraska wind.

Racks of peanuts and other snacks were prominently displayed. Several large jars with boiled eggs and spicy pickles sat on the bar enticing customers. A big cash register rang when the drawer was opened to make change. The bartenders were always busy washing the glasses, drawing draft beers, and talking to their customers. Sometimes I saw the bartenders make the beer red by pouring tomato juice into the beer. Every so often, I even saw them put a raw egg into the beer glass and serve it. Seeing that always turned my stomach.

Across from the bar were tables and chairs. People played cards at those tables and shared the latest town and farm stories. In the back half of the pool hall there were a lot of pool tables. Some had pockets for the balls to drop into, and some did not. Special games like billiards were played on the table without pockets, in which you tried to hit two red balls with the cue ball. Above the green tables, long lights hung low. Racks along the walls held cue sticks of varying lengths and chalk for the cue tips. Across the pool tables, wires were strung with beads for scorekeeping that slid back and forth as the pool players sank balls on the table. Tall columns stood in a line down the center of the room holding up the floor above the pool hall. The patterned tin ceiling was high and had rotating ceiling fans. The room was usually filled with loud talk and laughter and dense blue smoke swirled in the air.

Dad usually played pool for several hours. So sometimes I got to pal around with my cousin Ronnie. My Uncle Cecil (Ronnie's dad) worked in the pool hall.

One day as Ronnie and I were chasing each other up and down Webster Street, Ronnie ran into the pool hall. He opened the big door, which had a large pane of glass in it, and slammed it behind him to slow down my progress in the chase. I, however, did not stop. My hand and wrist went through the window.

I slashed my left wrist, and blood was gushing out. My dad came quickly to my aid and hurried me off to Dr. Obert with my wrist tightly bandaged. Dr. Obert whistled a tune as he sewed my wrist shut. It was not a good afternoon; it was my first time getting stitches. I still have the scar on my arm where I wear my wristwatch. My mom was not happy as we rode the eight miles north and half a mile west back home to the farm with my newly stitched wrist. Neither was I.

The Ice House

One of the items we bought each time we went to town during warm weather months was ice. In the first year or so on the north farm, we had an icebox to keep our food cool. The icebox was a heavily built cabinet made from oak. It had several doors with heavy brass hinges and latches. The whole inside was lined with tin or galvanized metal. The walls of the icebox and doors were a couple inches thick. A large chunk of ice went into one of the top compartments of the icebox.

Red Cloud had an ice plant on the northeast side of Cedar Street and 3rd. We always pulled into the drive of the ice plant near the loading dock.

Dad placed an order for the number of blocks of ice he wanted. Men moved around behind big, heavy curtains into a cavernous room. The men had large tongs with sharp points on each end of the tong. The tong was made to reach across the blocks of ice stored down in the pit of the room.

As I recall, the stored ice was insulated with wood shavings or straw. A block of ice was lifted with tongs and carried out to the car. Dad wrapped the ice block with burlap. The wet, wrapped ice went in the trunk of our '37 Chevy; sometimes it was placed on the floor in the back, which meant that we kids could put our feet on the cold wet burlap. In summer weather, the ice block made for a great travel treat as we drove home.

In the winter months, we got our ice for the icebox from our cattle tank. We chopped chunks of ice from the water in the livestock tank then refilled the tank using the windmill pump. We used the icebox year round. Leaving our food on the porch in winter would have frozen the food into rock hard lumps!

On one trip into town, we learned that the ice plant had burned down. (How does an ice plant burn? I guess it was the wood structure and wood shavings that packed the ice to keep it from melting.) No more ice in the summer!

My parents went to the appliance store and purchased a refrigerator that ran on kerosene. When the store delivered the refrigerator, I was excited to see how this new appliance made cold air from kerosene that burned hot. The man from the store opened a compartment at the bottom and slid out a flat tank with a round kerosene burner on the back corner. He filled the tank with kerosene and lit the burner's round wick. The round burner made a nice blue flame. The man from the store slid the tank and its lit burner back into the compartment and closed the compartment door. Later that day the refrigerator was cold inside. I thought it was magic that a kerosene burner could make things cold. Each day we added more kerosene so that the burner could make cold air in the refrigerator. We were able to put all kinds of food inside the new, white refrigerator.

Remembering Others

Every Memorial Day, we drove into town and went to Grandpa Hesman's house dressed in our church clothes. We picked flowers and filled quart jars of water. Sometimes Uncle Fred and Aunt Irene and my cousins met us at Grandpa's place. Midmorning all of us drove to the Red Cloud Cemetery. Many cars were parked along the little roads that circled through the cemetery grounds. We always wound our way through the cars to where Grandma Hesman was buried.

We put the flowers in the water-filled jars and set the flowers on the side of the reddish colored Hesman headstone. Grandma's name was the only name on the headstone. One day Grandpa knew his name would be engraved alongside Grandma's name. Grandpa opened the car door and just sat in the car and looked at the headstone for a long time.

Mom, Dad, and the rest of us looked around at the many headstones, flowers, and people remembering their past loved ones. I always made my way around the cemetery to see the most intriguing headstones. One tall headstone looked like two large tree trunks with vines that coiled around and up the tall trunks. The headstone was a foot taller than any man. The strange headstone had beauty and mystery about it.

Finally, marching men could be heard entering the cemetery with someone calling out the commands for the men dressed in military uniforms carrying rifles. Flag bearers led the men with the guns. A crowd gathered around the tall Civil War statue in the center of the cemetery. The flag bearers lined up in front of the statue. The seven American Legion Veteran Soldiers with guns lined up on the edge of the circle around the statue and raised their rifles. The commands: "Ready," the soldiers lifted their guns; "Aim," the rifles went to the soldiers' shoulder; and "Fire," the guns sounded off with white puffs of smoke shooting out of the muzzles into the air. Then, the soldiers reloaded the gun chambers. The commands "Ready, Aim, and Fire" were given three times total for a twenty-one-gun salute. Off in the distance could be heard the lonely bugle sound of

"taps." (Later during my teen years, the bugler would be my fellow Boy Scout friend.) After "taps," the American Legion Veterans followed the commands and marched back out of the cemetery. The crowd slowly dispersed back to their loved ones' gravesites for one more moment. Soon all the cars made their way back out of the cemetery and onto the Red Cloud streets.

    We always went back to Grandpa Hesman's house to have dinner together. In the mid-afternoon, my cousins left with my aunt and uncle. My family drove back to the farm. Grandpa stayed home alone.

chapter ten
big changes on the farm

In the summer we had lots of things to do. On the weekends or holidays, we went to Superior, where my cousin Waunie Lee lived. There all the Hager family had family picnics. Or maybe the picnics were held at my grandparents' house or at the Red Cloud City Park. All the aunts, uncles, and cousins attended. The potluck food covered the tables. Yes, my grandmother's baked beans were always on the table. I could just stuff myself on those beans!

Sometimes the family get-together was at our farm. The food was always abundant as the grownups outdid themselves. After the meal, watermelon was served. The kids stood outside to eat the slices of watermelon to the rind and to practice their seed spitting techniques. Often, the men or larger boys cranked the ice cream maker while the smaller kids added the salt onto the ice to make the ice colder. When the crank could no longer be turned, the ice cream crank and paddle were removed. A wet, burlap sack was wrapped around the bucket, ice, and ice cream to keep it frozen until the ice cream was served. All the while, the kids played games, explored in the barn, and rode the bikes. Trixie kept busy hauling us all around the farm. When the evening came, everyone went home. The chores still had to be done.

The Bulldozer

Late in the summer season, my dad and brother harvested all the wheat and corn. The alfalfa was cut and stacked near the cattle feeding lots. At the end to the harvest season, surveyors arrived at the farm; they started surveying and placing flags across all our fields.

Apparently the Government Farm Loans required and/or

provided a government erosion prevention program. The fields had ditches and ravines that left scars down the slopes of our fields from years of erosion. The topsoil washed away, leaving the poorer clay soil behind. The productivity of that soil was minimal. Preparing the soil, planting, and harvesting were difficult due to the rough terrain.

Soon bulldozers and road graders were unloaded and moved onto the fields. The bulldozers began to cut ditches into the hills: not down the hills, but around the hills. The road graders were used to carefully grade the soil so that there were terraces winding around the hillside all at the same level. Each hillside in each field had several terraces. The terraces held the topsoil and the moisture from rain on the hillside instead of running into the creek bottoms. After school, I loved to hurry home and watch these big machines reshape the land. I wished I could ride on those big machines. But I was afraid to ask the operators of the machines whether I could have a ride. The fields looked so different with those curving ribbons of soil wrapping around the hillsides of our farm. As the work was completed, the machines left; except for one lone bulldozer.

The bulldozer made its way across our pasture to the farthest northeast corner of our farm. At that spot, a creek bed came into our pasture from the farm on the other side of Highway 281. The operator started to push the dirt down the creek bed. He stopped pushing the dirt about a hundred yards away. The next day after school, I rode my bike on the cow paths all the way to where the bulldozer was working. The operator had made a deep hole and a high mound of dirt that filled the ravine from hill to hill. When I sat down to watch the man operate his machine, he stopped the bulldozer. He motioned for me to come to the bulldozer. When I stood at the side of the giant machine, I could not see the topside of the tracks of the dozer. He climbed down onto the tracks and gave me his hand. He pulled me up onto the tracks and helped me get up onto the big seat. He got back onto the seat and pushed the machine into gear. Wow!

The deafening noise of the engine, the black exhaust shooting out of the top of the engine into the sky, and the squeaking of metal on metal as the track rollers moved against the heavy steel track of the dozer was frightening and exciting. The earth seemed to melt in front of that giant blade. The big machine lurched and heaved as the blade went from soft soil to hard clay. As we pushed the dirt out of the hole, we started up the slope of the earthen dam. It seemed like we were going to tip over backwards. I could only see blue sky over the huge hood of the bulldozer. The dirt piled up over the top of the blade. Suddenly, the dozer lurched over the top edge of the dam and tipped down to the level surface that was created along the top of the dam. The man lifted his blade and put the dozer in reverse and down the slope we went with the tracks clattering as we traveled. I rode the bulldozer with a big smile on my face for several more times up the side of the dam. I wished my family could see me high on the seat of the huge yellow dozer. Then it was over.

The man let me off the bulldozer and told me goodbye. I watched until I thought I had to go home to do chores. At school I could hardly wait to get home so I could go back out to the bulldozer. When I got to the new dam, the man and his bulldozer were gone. The dam was completed. Water from the creek was already creating a pool of water in the bottom of the dam. With memories of that exciting ride the day before, I rode home to do my chores.

The Gift

One of the Saturdays before Christmas, we went into Red Cloud. Mom and I window-shopped, as we often did. Rarely did we buy anything. This time when we walked in front of the Gambles Hardware store, I spotted a toy road grader just like the ones that had created the terraces on our fields. We stopped and looked at that big orange road grader. I knew it must cost a lot of money. We walked on down the chilly, snowy sidewalk to our car and waited for the rest of the family.

Several weeks later, Christmas Eve came. It was our custom

to do chores, get cleaned up, and then open our Christmas gifts.

The farm landscape was covered with windblown snow. We had our Christmas tree up. Our family gathered together in the warmth of our living room heated by the fuel oil stove. The usual gifts were being given out: socks, under clothing, a coat. One gift remained behind the tree. Mom asked me to get the gift. She said it was mine.

I tore the wrapping off. Yes! That big orange road grader with its six large black rubber tires, front wheels that turned from the steering wheel, and a swiveling blade appeared out of the wrapping. I could not believe that I had received such a gift. When the spring thaw came, my grader and I moved lots of dirt into roads out behind the chicken coop.

The City

An exciting time for a farm boy was when I got to go to Hastings, Nebraska and stay with my cousin Ronnie. Hastings was a real city compared to the towns in Webster County. My Aunt Opal, Uncle Cecil, and Ronnie lived in a housing complex on the east side of Hastings.

I remember playing with Ronnie's metal trucks. We played in the housing complex playground. My Aunt Opal took us around Hastings when she went on her errands. *We had no chores*. We just played all the time.

One night, we were awakened by Ronnie's mother. She was scared. She heard a noise outside her bedroom window. When she pulled back the curtain, she stared into the face of a man outside her window. When the man saw that she had seen him, he ran away. My aunt called the police. Ronnie and I found a baseball bat in the closet. We packed that ball bat around to ward off any burglars or peeping Toms from our apartment. The police investigation found that the intruder had stuck a wire through the screen and tried to unlatch the screen so he could lift the window to get in. I was unnerved because I did not know about crime and life in the city.

The Gnat

Another time I stayed with my other cousins. My parents were gone on a trip, so I stayed with Uncle Fred and Aunt Irene. Their farm was fifteen miles north of Red Cloud and about a mile west. We did all the farming chores that I was used to when I stayed with this family.

Uncle Fred had Ford tractors. They were fun to drive. They were low and had wide front wheels. Fords were more like driving a car compared to my dad's John Deere, which was tall and had narrow front wheels.

One day we hooked a wagon behind the tractor. We put rolls of barbed wire and tools into the wagon. We drove the tractor down a cow lane to the spot where the fence needed repairing. We strung new barbed wire from post to post. We used rope and pulley wire stretchers. When the wire was tight, we hammered wire staples into the posts. We strung three barbed wires onto the posts to make a good cattle fence.

It was a warm and steamy morning for working. The gnats were out flying all around our heads and eyes. I tried to swish the gnats away with my hand. They were persistent.

One gnat flew into my ear and stuck to my ear drum. That gnat sounded like an elephant stomping on my brain. I could not get the gnat to leave my ear. I started yelling to everyone that I had a gnat in my ear. I was carrying on pretty badly. Uncle Fred was concerned, but I think he thought I was pretty funny. We drove back to the house on the tractor. The gnat continued to tromp the heck out my ear drum. Aunt Irene put water down my ear canal and tried to wipe the gnat out of my ear. Finally, silence. For the rest of my stay at my relatives farm, I was reminded how funny I was with the gnat in my ear. My uncle Fred talked about my gnat experience many times later.

The My Antonia *Farm*

Every so often, Grandpa Hesman drove out to our farm. Then, we all drove north on Highway 281 to the fourteen-mile corner. There, we turned west onto Highway 4 for a mile and then turned back south for part of a mile. My Great Aunt Helen and Great Uncle Jim Bouska lived on the farm that became well known because of Willa Cather's novel *My Antonia*; the farm house was purchased in 1976 by the Cather Foundation and now the house is on the Federal Register of Historic Places.

At my age, the notoriety of the farm being described in a book did not mean much. But, from time to time the subject of a famous author from Red Cloud, who wrote about her childhood visits to the house, would come up among the grownups. Aunt Helen Nohavec Bouska was my grandmother Carrie Nohavec Hesman's younger sister. The Bouskas, Nohavecs, and Hesmans were all Bohemian, as were many of the farmers around that part of Webster County.

Most of the time when we visited Aunt Helen and Uncle Jim, my Aunt Irene and Uncle Fred along with my cousins Victor, Bob, and Judy, came to visit as well. We were greeted by Aunt Helen, Uncle Jim, and their grown-up son, Lad.

After our greetings, we went onto the enclosed front porch where all the well-used farm clothing was hung. Milk buckets, garden tools, and other items that were regularly needed for chores filled the long porch. From the porch, the kitchen was directly ahead. The big cob stove was straight across the room. It was always hot and covered with kettles. Traffic-patterned, worn linoleum covered the kitchen floor. They had a sink and a hand pump right in the kitchen and enough kitchen cabinets to hide most of the dishes and cooking items.

The kitchen, without a doubt, smelled like kolaches. Kolaches are round, chewy pastries filled in the center indentation with fruit filling. Normally, our eyes would gaze onto a low table next to the stove where cherry, peach, prune, apricot, and poppy seed kolaches were cooling from just being baked. We kids did not dare to snatch a kolache before they were served, which was whenever Aunt Helen decided it was time. If we were having dinner, the kolaches cooled until after the meal. If it was a Sunday afternoon drop-in gathering, we might be served kolaches when the coffee was hot and ready to be served. Aunt Helen always had enough kolaches to feed all the grown-ups and us kids till we were stuffed, maybe up to four each!

The living room was to the left of the kitchen in the main part of the house. The men made their way into the living room, and Aunt Helen started her kitchen work so the food or pastries and coffee were just right for serving. Aunt Irene and Mom pitched in to the extent Aunt Helen allowed. The grown-ups talked about the weather; how the crops did during the last rain or lack of rain; how close the recent tornado or hail storm was; whether there was enough hay to last the winter; if all the calves made it through the spring; if the alfalfa was ready to be cut; or how all the members of the family were holding up.

At the beginning of a visit, we kids might listen to the conversation, but slowly we disappeared to explore more exciting options. If the weather was nice, we played out to the side of the house on the cellar mound. We kept a lookout for the big white aggressive geese. They were good at getting close enough that they charged us and grabbed us with their beaks. If they bit to the skin, the pinch really hurt.

To the north of the house and across the driveway, fruit trees grew. Here and there were berry bushes. There were crab apple trees, peach trees, cherry trees, apricot trees, and mulberry trees. The orchard area of the farm was different because no one else I knew had an orchard with so many varieties of fruit in their own yard. We spent time in the orchard and picked ripe fruit off the trees, if it was in season.

Sometimes we explored the equipment buildings or the huge barn at the other end of the farmyard. We might throw some grain to the chickens to see them scramble for the most seed. We never went too far away or stayed out too long. It would have been a tragedy to miss the kolaches.

I really did not know much about my Great Aunt and Uncle. I knew they were hard working farmers. The demanding toil of farm life could be seen on Aunt Helen's face. She always wore a button-up dress and looked tired. Uncle Jim wore thick round glasses that made his eyes look larger than they were. He wore a long sleeved shirt and high waisted pants with suspenders like Grandpa Hesman. He had only one hand. On his left arm he had a chrome pincher that he could open and close. He seemed to be just as effective at holding and moving things as I was with my hands. I tried not to stare; but he was the first person I knew who had a mechanical hand. Their son Lad wore faded blue overalls and a white T-shirt. He had a dark complexion from the sun. Both Uncle Jim and Lad had white foreheads where their hats protected their skin from the sun.

At the end of our visits, we said our goodbyes. We usually only got together about every six months.

The Carnivals

In the fall, lots of carnivals came to the little Midwest towns of Nebraska. My family often went to these exciting events in Red Cloud, Blue Hill, or Bladen. The carnivals always had exciting rides like the huge Ferris wheel, the Octopus, and swings on long chains that swung out and around. Of course, the carnivals had Merry-Go-Rounds and other small kid rides. The carnival alleys were lined with various games such as darts, shooting galleries, coin tosses into carnival glass dishes, floating ducks swimming round and round in the water, and stacked bottles waiting to be knocked over by a baseball. Booth after booth was filled with desirable carnival toy prizes: swords; pin wheels; and stick canes topped with animal heads, ceramic dice, or fancy figurines. There were stands filled with scrumptious delights like cotton candy, fried dough with powder sugar, hot dogs, ice cream dipped in chocolate and nuts, candied apples, popcorn, and all kinds of goodies to make one's tummy sick on those chilly fall evenings.

As one moved through the carnival, the air was filled with all kinds of music playing at the various booths and rides. The unmistakable sounds of the carnival created sheer excitement for a young boy who rarely left his farm, except to go to Red Cloud on Sale Days and Saturdays to get our weekly provisions.

Sometimes at the carnival, there were colorful side shows that had freakish pictures painted on the large booths. The pictures were of things like an extremely tall person, an extremely fat lady, a very small person, a calf with two heads, or a cat with five legs. There were pictures of an elephant person, a mummy from Egypt, and a shrunken head that head-hunters made.

And, I particularly remember a frightening picture of an alligator with a human head.

The alligator picture on the front of the show stuck in my mind as the most unusually scary thing to see. I never thought an alligator could have a human head! Quite frankly, I had not thought much of alligators at all. I had seen grotesque snapping turtles, but never alligators in Nebraska.

In front of the sideshow, a man or woman sat in a little ticket booth to sell tickets that allowed people to go inside to see the scary, amazing carnival show. Many people lined up the ramp and went inside. I was not old enough to actually go inside. When they came out the other side and down the ramp, it seemed they looked stunned from seeing the oddities of nature they had just witnessed. I was not sure I would ever want to see what they had seen.

The Chores Increase for a Farm Boy

As I aged, my chores increased and got harder. Not only did I have to get the eggs from the chicken houses, gather cobs for the cook stove, and carry water to the house, but I had to feed the calves milk and turn the cream separator crank when we separated the cream from the cow's milk. But wait, there's more! There was intermittent work such as pushing hay out of the hayloft to the cows in their milk stalls. If the cows did not come into the barn on their own, I went into the pasture with Blackie and herded the cows back to the barn. I helped my parents pitchfork the muck out of the cow's stalls and take it outside. I had to throw ears of corn from the corncrib into the pig pen. I had household chores as well, like drying the dishes with my sister.

Gathering Cobs

I am sure there were other duties, but the one that sticks in my mind as the hardest chore was gathering cobs for the cook stove. There were two ways we got cobs on a farm. The easiest way was when we shelled our corn for livestock feed in the fall.

The ears of corn were fed through a corn sheller. The sheller was a dangerous machine that was driven by a long belt connected to the tractor's belt drum. The ears of corn were put into a hopper on top of the sheller. Out of the sheller came kernels of corn, and out the other side, the clean cobs fell to the ground. I was not allowed to be near the sheller when it was running. It made a horrible noise when the ears were fed to the sheller. The kernels of corn were collected to be crushed or used as whole kernels. The nice clean cobs were stored in a wire cob crib that looked like a storage tank, but was made of woven wire instead of sheet metal.

When those cobs were used in the winter, I had to rake the cobs out of the bottom of the cob crib into a bushel basket. Sometimes snow and ice made it hard to get the cobs to fall down into my basket. The cob crib was way out behind the barn. So I carried the basket by hand or balanced the basket on my wagon all the way into the house. This was not an easy task, because the yard was muddy or crisscrossed with frozen ruts from the car and tractors coming and going. At the house, the cobs were dumped into a box near the stove.

The harder way to get cobs was to throw the ears of corn from the corncrib into the pigpen. The pigs ate the kernels of corn off the cobs. The cobs became buried in the mud and were covered with what pigs leave in the mud—pig poo. It was my job to enter the pigpen, avoid the angry mother pig with her piglets, and kick the cobs loose from the mud. If the ground was frozen, I got the cobs from the cob crib. If I could get the cobs loose from the mud, I filled the basket and took the basket to the house. Cobs covered with mud are a lot heavier than clean cobs. The dried, but dirty cobs, burned in the cook stove just as well as the clean cobs. The fire was always started with the clean cobs. A little kerosene was poured on the cobs to help them light faster.

The secret to this chore was to never run out of clean cobs before the winter had ended. If you did not plan well and the weather was freezing, it was impossible to get cooking fuel from cobs frozen in the mud. Successfully monitoring the amount of clean cobs was my way of getting hot meals and escaping the wrath of my mother. Oh yes, another chore was scooping the ashes out of the bottom of the cook stove and carrying the ashes to the chickens. The chickens liked the ashes.

We always made sure to take good care of the chickens. They were an important part of farm life. One day a near disaster occurred when one of the heaters that kept the little chicks warm in the chicken house tipped over and started a fire inside the chicken house. The fire happened at a time that it was noticed right away. By the time we got the fire put out, the walls in one part of the small building were charred. The outcome was interesting. Just like the cob stove ashes, the chickens loved the black char in their house; they pecked the black charred wood completely away as high as they could reach.

Taming Weeds

Each spring I joined the rest of my family to cut down bad weeds that grew in the pastures and along the edges of newly planted fields. The weeds were a problem because they crowded out the pasture grass, and if cows ate them, the cow's milk had a bitter taste. Together we walked along and looked for sunflowers, milkweed, sting nettles, and thistles. If we cut the weeds down before they bloomed, the reseeding of those weeds decreased each year. We each wielded a machete. We hacked each weed down with our big sharp blades. I cut down the small ones. The milk from the milkweed gave us rashes; the stinging nettles burned our skin if we brushed up against them, and the thistles had pointed thorns on the stocks and blooms, which stuck in our skin and clothes. It was dangerous work. We kept a safe distance from each other to avoid getting hit by another person's machete.

One day, we were whacking down sunflowers. Suddenly, my dad made a frightful sound. He pulled up his pants leg and revealed a big gash. His machete missed the sunflower stock and hit his leg. We went back to the house immediately. Mom cleaned up the wound. I do not remember dad going to the doctor; I guess with Mom's care the deep cut healed on its own. He was lucky to not have been injured more seriously.

Mixing Ensilage

In the spring and summer our cows roamed the pasture for grass. In the winter we threw them hay. The other main source of cattle feed was ensilage. Ensilage was made from hay, straw, and chopped corn stocks. The whole mix was called fodder. The sugars of the corn were released in the fermenting process. The fermentation was caused from the heat and pressure that built up in the fodder. One might wonder how we got fermented ensilage. It was not easy.

We started by finding a steep bank near the pasture, not far from the cornfield. Dad dug a deep trench from the topside of the bank down to the surface on the lower side of the bank. The trench was deeper than the height of our tractor. The trench bottom rose from the lower level of the bank to the top ground surface fifty to seventy feet in length. The trench was cleaned out so it had a nice smooth floor. The walls were made straight.

The long open trench became our silo. Wire mesh was laid in the wagon prior to loading. The fodder was loaded on top of the wire mesh. Dad drove the tractor, with the full wagon of raw fodder, down into the trench. The second tractor, driven by my brother, was hitched with a rope to the far end of the wire mesh. As my father drove along the trench, the fodder dropped out of the wagon onto the floor of the trench. As more loads were dumped, the fodder became deeper in the trench. The fodder was compacted by driving the second tractor back and forth over the fodder. The process of filling the dirt silo ended when the compacted fodder filled the trench to the top.

My job in all this was to sit on the bank and watch the action. One day, my brother, Ken, was driving the tractor back and forth in and out of the trench to compact the fodder. Dad was watching my brother from the upper side of the trench. As Ken backed down into the trench, the tractor's left wheel stayed on the bank and its right wheel started dropping down into the trench on the fodder. Soon the tractor was leaning precariously to one side. The front tires on the tractor were side-by-side under the nose of the tractor. There was nothing to prevent the tractor from tipping over. Sure enough, over it went, throwing my brother out to the side. My dad pretty much caught Ken in mid-air as the tractor rolled over onto the fodder.

I ran to the house screaming for Mom and Barb. When the whole family got together at the silo, my parents sized up the situation. My brother was not hurt. Dad took the other tractor and hitched a chain to the overturned tractor and pulled. The fallen tractor rolled back onto its wheels. The only damage to the uprighted tractor seemed to be a bent exhaust pipe. The tractor was refueled and restarted to continue its work.

When the trench was finally full, a tarp was spread out to cover the whole top surface of the fodder. Tires and rocks were put on top of the tarp to hold it in place. In the following winter, the tarp at the bottom of the ditch was pulled back. Warm, steaming ensilage was available for the cattle to eat. They loved it.

Milking Cows

When the cows are full, they are happy. When cows are happy, they give more milk. A cow's udders fill with milk each morning and evening. I thought it must be difficult for the cows to have those heavy milk bags swinging back and forth between their back legs. But they seemed to manage.

When the barn door opened, the cows eagerly entered the barn. They were especially eager if it was cold and blowing snow outside. Inside, each cow found a stall. Dad shoved them around so all the stalls filled up with the large warm bodies. We threw hay down to the cows from the hayloft. Each cow chewed the hay and then contentedly chewed their cud. Cud is the regurgitated food from the cow's first stomach which is re-chewed slowly, then swallowed into the second stomach of the cow. The cows seemed to enjoy the second opportunity to chew their food. We shackled each cow's back legs so they could not kick or move around while being milked. My parents gave the cows instructions by name when they needed to be maneuvered around inside the barn. I could never tell if the cows actually knew their own names. The area of the barn that the cows were in quickly became warm from their body heat.

Mom, Dad, and my brother milked the cows. Mom tried to teach me to milk the cows, but I was not strong enough to get any milk to squirt out. It takes strong hands to squeeze and pull down on the nipple at the same time.

The three milkers crouched between the cows and under the back side of the cow waiting to be milked. The milker's head was placed against the lower back side of the cow's stomach. While sitting on a one legged stool, holding the bucket between one's knees, the milker squeezed and pulled down on two nipples of the udder. The milk squirted into the bucket making a spraying sound. It was necessary to use both hands for efficiency.

The rhythm to milking was important. When I listened, there was a right squirt, pause, left squirt, pause, right squirt, pause, etc. I think there was some sort of harmony between the cow and the milker. The sound of several milkers squirting the milk into the buckets was like music not heard by many people.

When the sound of milking filled the barn, the cats showed up one by one. They loved to get squirted in the face with cow's milk so they could lick the milk off their whiskers. When the harmony got disrupted, let's say by a fly tickling the cow on the utter, the cow moved to the side, flicked her tail, or worse, she might knock the partially filled bucket to the ground. And even worse, she might knock the milker onto the dirty barn floor. No one dared to laugh at the fuming mad, angry fallen milker. When that happened, the whole evening was ruined, especially if it was my mom who landed on the barn floor.

Getting knocked over and spilling the milk was not only embarrassing, but the milk was spilled. The milk was a source of income, food for the calves, and food for our family. We may not have had much money, but we always had plenty to eat: milk and cream from our cows, eggs from our chickens, produce from our garden, and meat from our livestock.

Milk Processing

The milk was carried from the barn and poured into the tank on top of a milk-processing machine, called a separator. Like much of the farm machinery, the separator was human powered. Someone turned the crank handle, which made the separator discs spin. The machine used centrifugal force to separate the heavy cream from the thin milk. As the milk flowed through the spinning discs, the thicker cream spun off from the thinner milk. Cream flowed out one spout into a cream can and the milk flowed from another spout into a milk can. Some of the cream was then churned into butter. Each time we used the separator, it was carefully disassembled, thoroughly washed, and reassembled. This chore had to be done each day. Our family saved enough milk and cream for our own needs.

Meat Processing

Having meat available for our family was not as easy as it may sound. Meat processing was best begun on a cold day to prevent disease in the meat. It was Dad's job to choose the right animal and herd it into the barn. All I ever heard was a rifle shot; I never watched the kill. The animal was bled and then hoisted up on a rope pulley in the barn. Dad skinned the hide off and removed the entrails. The entrails released vapor as the warm pile was exposed to the cold air in the barn. The brain, liver, heart, and tongue were put in a bucket for a special use. The body of the pig or cow was quartered and wrapped in burlap. Dad put the quartered animal in the car and took it to the butcher. After the butcher cut the animal into the right cuts of meat, the packaged meat was put into a frozen meat locker. Each time we went to town, we went into the cold meat locker and chose the cuts of meat to bring home. We took only enough packages of frozen meat to last us until our next trip to town.

Farm Style Eating

The saved brain, liver, heart, and tongue were taken to the house. Each one was cooked a special way to make it the most palatable. The brains were mixed with eggs and eaten at breakfast. I never touched the stuff. The liver was fried with onions and eaten with catsup. Mom served mashed potatoes and gravy with the liver and onions for supper. That was one of my favorite meals. The heart and tongue were sliced and used in sandwiches. Pickles, mayonnaise, mustard, or catsup were added to the sandwich. I was okay with the sandwiches, but most of the time I tried to avoid eating them. The meat was kind of crunchy.

My favorite farm meal was ground up, fried beef with mashed potatoes and gravy, served along with pork and beans. I mixed the pork and beans in with the mashed potatoes and gravy. Then, I flattened the heap of food down into imaginary roads and ate them. I suppose it was a boy thing. I made Mom and my sister mad when I made roads in my food.

One night I saw my dad put some white stuff all over his meat. I asked him what that white stuff was. He said it was horseradish, and it tasted good. He put a big pile of the horseradish on my meat. I cut a piece of meat off with a large amount of horseradish on it. When the horseradish hit my mouth, I thought I was eating something from hell. My sinuses exploded like a dropped watermelon. My eyes watered like the windmill pump. I spit it out onto my plate and headed for the water pail in the sink. I hung my tongue into the water-filled ladle that we used to dip water out of the water bucket. My family laughed at me, Mom consoled me, and I cried out that my dad tricked me. After a time, I eventually learned to like the spicy tang of horseradish.

Castrating Calves

My uncle visited our farm each spring to help us with a delicate livestock procedure. We kids were instructed to gather all the male calves into the corral. Those cute little critters did not know what was coming. A farm only needs one or two bulls. The young want-to-be bulls were destined to be steers instead; one day they would be meat for the table.

Once all the calves were cornered, they ran into a chute that held them tight. I stood on the fence and watched. Dad had his sharp knife ready. With a flick of Dad's knife and in the blink of an eye, the calf was castrated and had no jewels. A black tar-like substance was put on the wound, and the calf was let go. After each calf's nightmare, the little guys ran around and kicked up their back feet for several minutes; then they moved slowly back to the pastures. For dinner that night, mom fried those little round things and sliced them so they fit nicely on bread for sandwiches. People call steer testicles Rocky Mountain oysters. My family liked them, but after being made to taste one, I elected to go without meat for those meals.

Maintaining The Water Source

Water was important for not only the animals, but for our family. Our farm had a well that was located closer to the barn than to the house. A tall, galvanized metal windmill stood over the well. A large bladed wheel and a weather vane topped the windmill. A lever at ground level lifted up so the brake on the bladed wheel could be released. When the brake was released, the weather vane turned the bladed wheel into the oncoming breeze. Slowly the wheel turned until it reached its proper speed. Gears attached to the bladed wheel made a long wooden pole go up and down. The long pole attached to the pump at ground level. As the cam lifted the pole, the pump plunger siphoned water out of the deep well.

The pump discharged the water to either a tank where the horses and cows drank or to the cistern. The cistern was a brick-lined, dirt-bottomed tank in the ground. The dirt bottom of the cistern allowed ground water to partially fill the underground chamber from below. On top of the cistern, there was a hand pump. If the handle of the pump was lifted up and down, the water flowed out from the hand pump. When the wind did not blow hard enough to turn the windmill, the livestock tank and the cistern provided enough reserve water until the wind blew again.

One day Mom and Dad decided the water from the cistern tasted bad. My dad took the boards off the top of the cistern. Using a mirror, Dad reflected the light down into the deep, dark cavity. Sure enough, things were floating and moving down in the water. Dad lit a lantern and lowered it down to just above the water level. Harmful gases did not extinguish the flame, therefore Dad knew there was enough oxygen for someone to safely go down into the cistern.

Dad got one of the barn ladders and positioned it in the cistern so he could climb down to the water level. We used a rope to lift up some boards that had dropped from the cistern cover down into the water. Then we lowered a bucket down so that he could catch the frogs and salamanders that were swimming around. When Dad thought he had everything removed that was making the drinking water foul, he climbed out. We covered the cistern top with new boards. For several days we let the windmill pump fill the cistern to overflowing. After this cleansing and purging of the well water, the cistern water was safe to drink again.

This was an important lesson for me, because it was my job

to carry water to the house. In fact, everyone carried water to the house at some point. It was a never-ending job. If a breeze was blowing and the windmill was pumping water to the livestock tank or cistern, I opened the pump valve to fill my bucket. If the windmill was not running, I lifted the brake lever to get running water from the windmill pump. When my bucket was full, I pushed the brake lever down so the windmill stopped pumping. If there was no breeze, I had to lift the cistern pump handle up and down to get the water to flow into my bucket. That was always harder.

Normally, I used two covered pails. I put them into my wagon and pulled the load to the house. Depending on the activities of the day, I might make several trips to the windmill for water.

When my parents were not watching, I climbed the windmill. On one of the legs of the tower, hand/footholds stuck out. Those hand/footholds were necessary for the maintenance of the windmill bearings and gears, but I used them for climbing as high as I could. Besides the height of the tower, the whirring sound of the turning blades of the windmill up near the top of the tower made it all the more exciting. It was not as hazardous as it sounds because there was a small platform at the top of the tower to prevent a person from being hit by the blades and wind vane.

The prize of the climb was the view out across the farm for what seemed like miles. I saw my dad and brother on the tractor tilling or planting the fields. I saw my sister on one of the horses heading out into the pasture to herd the cows home. I saw the cars and trucks heading up and down Highway 281. I saw the cloud of dust chase a car as it passed by our farm. I saw both creeks on each side of the hill on which our farmyard was located. I saw into our neighbor's farm on the south side of our dirt road. It seemed like I was on top of the world and saw it all in motion.

The Rural Electrification Project

One spring day in 1951 while riding our bikes home from school, we kids noticed men and trucks with augers and poles working along the road. Each day the poles, one by one, were set into the ground. Cross arms with glass knobs topped each pole. The poles were set every hundred feet or so up and down the hills along the road. Then, trucks with large spools of wire arrived. From pole to pole, the workmen strung a couple wires. The existing telephone wires were moved and attached to the new poles, and the smaller telephone poles were removed.

Men with sharp spikes attached to the sides of their boots installed the polls and wires with expert efficiency. They each had a long belt that went around their waist and then around the pole that they were to climb. The belt was thrown up the backside of the pole; the worker leaned back and stuck his spikes into the pole then stepped up onto the buried spike. Again the belt was thrown up, the other spike was stuck into the pole at a higher level, and the worker stepped up. This action repeated until the worker got to the top of the pole. There, perched at the top of the pole, one or two workers did their work. Finally, a pole was installed in front of our house. The workers installed something that looked like a tank on the pole. Out of that metal tank, called a transformer, a wire was strung across the yard and attached to our house. The Rural Electrification Project had come to our little farm and changed our lives.

After the line was installed into a meter box on our house, a man with a truck, ladders, wire, and all kinds of other items came to our house. He started using the power from the meter box to drill holes in the walls and all throughout the attic of our house. I felt it was my duty, when not in school, to watch this man do his work. Sometimes we went under the house. Most of the time, we were in the attic. He strung wires through the holes down into the walls and ceilings. Plugs and light fixtures were attached to the wires. A tall light was placed in the yard so we could see all the way to the barn at night.

While all the electrical work was being done, my parents bought some electrical items, such as lamps, light bulbs, a radio, an electric motorized tub washing machine with a power wringer for wringing out our clothes, and an electric clock for the wall. Later, we got an electric refrigerator and new fuel oil stove with an electric fan to better heat the house. Finally, the cob cook stove was replaced with an electric cook stove. (That was the end of gathering cobs!) The kerosene lamps in every room were no longer necessary; except for when the power went out. The clothes scrub board and tub were set aside. Life was good as we enjoyed the comforts of electricity.

The activities in the house changed as well. With electric lights, we got to stay up later in the evening. For the first time, we could see in our bedrooms early in the morning and after dark to dress or, God forbid, study in our room. We listened to radio shows like Red Skelton, Amos and Andy, and Abbott and Costello in our living room. We could listen to weather, news, music, boxing matches, and baseball games. It was a whole new way of life.

Just above the heating stove, a vent went through the living room ceiling to the upstairs hallway floor grate. That vent was the only source of heat for the upstairs. But also, it was a place where we kids could secretly listen to the radio programs from downstairs. If we sat near the grate, it was warm and entertaining even after bedtime.

Alligators Under My Bed

In the winter, our rooms upstairs became very cold. There was little to no insulation in the walls. Icy frost gathered on the windows. The beds needed a number of heavy blankets for us to keep warm. My big brother and I shared a bed and were constantly feuding about it. At night, I got cold and moved next to him to keep warm. He always insisted that there was an invisible line down the center of our bed and that I was not to cross the line. As the consequence for crossing the line, I got an elbow in the side. It always seemed unfair that he had plenty of heat on his side of the bed. Why not share some warmth with his little brother?

It was in our little upstairs room that I experienced a lifelong fear. From time to time, I was reminded of the alligator picture at the Carnival. I wondered whether alligators might be living somewhere in Nebraska. The question of where an alligator would hide, and how would it get a human head could not be answered in my child's brain

One night I had a nightmare about alligators hiding under my bed. The dream seemed so real to me. I knew there was something lurking under there. Maybe the alligator had come to get me. After the dream, I jumped off and away from the edge of my bed and ran downstairs. I told my mom that there might be an alligator under my bed.

My mom insisted that there were no alligators under my bed. I was not convinced. Also, when I told my brother about the alligators lurking under our bed, he did not give me the same assurance. Rather, he played up my fears to keep me in line.

Never again did I dangle my feet over the edge of the bed for fear of my toes and feet being chomped off.

chapter eleven
big changes for a nebraska boy

As the seasons and years went by on the farm, I grew enough to do more chores. My new strengths and talents put me in charge of my brother's chores, which freed my brother to do more of Dad's work on the farm. That is the way farm life worked.

Instead of watching my dad and brother cut and rake the hay, I was allowed to drive the John Deere tractor to pull the rake and hay wagon. The John Deere had the throttle on the steering column. The clutch was not activated by our feet, but instead was engaged by pushing a lever forward with our hand. If I sat on the edge of the seat with one hip, I could reach the break.

Also, I was strong enough to keep up with my sister on the old bicycle. We rode the half-mile to the west to get the mail on our bikes. We enhanced our bikes with playing cards held by clothespins on the frames of our bikes to make a motor sound.

Barb rode Trixie into the pasture while I kept up on my bike; together we rounded up the cattle out in the pasture. The cow paths that took us across the east creek into the pasture went right by a prairie dog community. Morning and evening, the alert prairie dogs would stand up on their hind legs and spot our approach. A barking alarm was sounded and every prairie dog disappeared in a flash. If we stopped, first one would stick his head out. If no harm was perceived, the prairie dog returned to the mound in front of the hole and stood up on his back legs to survey the creek and banks for possible danger. More and more dogs would appear to begin their community activities. In the spring, many pups could be spotted. They were always fun to watch, but farmers did not like the prairie dog colonies living in the pastures. If a cow or horse stepped in one of their holes, quite often it meant a broken leg for the cow or horse. Poison or rifles were used to reduce the thriving prairie dog colonies.

Bicycle Maintenance

The downside of riding my bike in the pasture was Texas Sand Burs. The burs were pointy and stuck in the tires of my bike, causing them to go flat. I had to fix my bike tires myself. I removed the wheel, tire, and tube. After adding some air into the tube, I held the tube under water in a bucket. When I saw bubbles flowing out of the tube, I knew where the hole was. Sometimes there were several holes. I marked each leak.

When we went to town, I bought tire patch kits at the Coast-To-Coast store. The patch kit's lid had a grater that was used to scuff the rubber where the hole was. Glue was spread around on the scuffed up spot. Then, the proper sized patch was applied to the glue spot and pressed. While the glue dried, I used my finger to feel around the inside of the tire. Most of the time, I felt the sharp point of the bur still sticking through the tire. I dug the bur out with an awl (a pointy metal tool). I made sure I got all the sharp points out. After for the drying time ended, the tube was placed back into the tire mounting. Once the bike was reassembled, I pumped the tires up to a firm level of pressure.

Bicycle tires can only be patched so many times though. Eventually I had to buy new tubes when we went to town. If the tires got a bulge or were too smooth, my parents bought me a new tire for my bike. Bikes were my thing, I loved to ride and maintain my ugly bike.

The Horses

Barb loved to ride the horses. Whenever there was a moment of time and for any reason, Barb put Trixie's bridle on and swung up onto Trixie's back to go riding. Trixie loved to run, and Barb encouraged Trixie's fastest capability.

Barb hid hay in her hand; Trixie came to Barb and bumped Barb with her nose until Barb gave her the prize. Barb was the one who Trixie depended on day in and day out. There was a true love between the young girl and her horse. One day Trixie got sick and suddenly died. That was a sad day for all of us, but it was even tougher for my sister because she lost a good companion. Trixie left a legacy; Barb always loved horses, rode horses, owned horses, and she even wrote children books about horses.

Ken sold his horse Queeny to buy his first car so he could drive to Cowles High School. His car was mighty fine; it was a black '36 Ford coupe. It had flared fenders, a large radiator, a tapered hood, a tilt-out windshield, running boards, and a long sloping back trunk. Because he had friends at Cowles High School, I did not see too much of Ken once he started driving. He was around just at chore time and bedtime so that we could feud over bed space.

The Hunt

Pheasant hunting became an activity that I was now eligible to participate in as an older youth. My uncles and cousins came to the farm for pheasant hunting. We went out into the fields and walked up the rows of grain. The pheasants would sneak along the rows for as long as they dared. Suddenly, two or three colorful pheasants would fly up into the air making that special flapping and squawking sound of alarm as they gained altitude and speed. Then, boom, boom, boom went the shotguns. Usually one or more birds dropped to the ground in a limp fall with feathers falling slowly behind them. The dead birds were stuffed into the large pockets of the grown-ups' hunting coats. The guns were reloaded. The march up the field commenced. I carried the small 4/10 shotgun. But, I never seemed to get any shots off because everything happened so fast. I was always being told what to do with my gun so we all stayed safe.

Sometimes we went rabbit hunting. The best rabbits to hunt were cottontails. The alternative was to hunt Jack Rabbits. Any dead rabbit was better than nothing. I was able to shoot the rabbits with my 4/10 shotgun. As I think back, I do not remember hitting any. But the hunt was fun. We went out to hunt when there were a few inches of snow on the ground. The rabbit tracks could easily be seen, and it was harder for the rabbits to run. They made long hops in the snow in a zigzag fashion to escape the hunter. The hunt usually resulted in four or five rabbits hanging on someone's belt. They made a good Sunday dinner.

Every once in a while a coyote was seen during our hunts. We always tried to shoot the coyotes because there was a bounty on coyote pelts. The coyotes killed young livestock and chickens. One morning my dad, brother, and I got up very early and drove just south of Blue Hill, Nebraska. Cars, pickups, and trucks were parked along the road as far as the eye could see. There were hundreds of hunters lined up along the fence line. Their guns were prepared for the hunt, and the hunters stood around sharing stories with each other. All were breathing the cold morning frost from their noses and mouths.

I was not given a gun; I was told to stay close to my dad. Soon the hunters started walking across the fields and pastures all in a row about fifty feet apart. Every so often the rapid firing of shotguns was heard from far off, but then closer to us, the gunshots started. Jack Rabbits jumped and ran until the buckshot hit its mark. We walked in close formation over the hills into gullies and draws. As we walked, the distance between the hunters became closer. The shotguns were heard and seen more and more. Finally, we reached the crown of a hill where hunters could be seen on both sides and at a distance on the left and on the right. Straight across from us there were hunters also.

In the center of the circle of hunters there were animals running here and there. The hunters were firing upon all the rabbits, foxes, and coyotes. It was a dangerous time; if an animal tried to run through the line of humans, the guns were aimed toward the fleeing animal, and sometimes at the other hunters. The hunters got mad if an inexperienced hunter violated the rules of safety.

After a while, the shooting stopped. Hopefully, no one was hit with buckshot.

The hunters collected the dead animals. The coyotes and foxes were hung on the sides of trucks. Jack Rabbits lay on the ground in piles. The hunters milled around drinking warmed coffee and maybe something stronger, while telling each other their stories. We had just participated in a coyote hunt.

All of the animals were considered a menace to the farmer because they ate grain, chickens, ducks, young calves, and piglets. There was a bounty paid for pelts, and the hunters enjoyed the hunt. I was cold, wet, and amazed at what I witnessed.

The Sled

Snow was a pain for farmers to endure. But the moisture was needed for the spring planting. As for us kids, we tried to make the most of the snow.

Out in the pasture was a steep hill with a few cow paths passing across the sloping hill. We had a wooden sled with runners that we used on this slope over the years. But, now that we were older, we were ready for higher levels of excitement. The old kerosene refrigerator was out in the area where we dumped unwanted things. My brother took the door off and unscrewed the inside shelves from the door. The door handle was removed. All three of us kids carried the long, curved shell of a door out to the top of the hill. We sized things up. Because the door was curved on the sides, the door would need to travel down the hill sideways. That meant all three of us sat side by side.

Barb and I sat in the door first; then, Ken gave the door a push and jumped in. The unusual sled started off pretty slow. As it gained speed, though, I got worried. Snow was kicking up into our faces. We were bouncing left and right. Then, we crossed a cow path. The sled dipped down and rose into the air. It slammed down onto the snow just in time for the next cow path. When the sled got to the bottom of the hill, I was still digging myself out of the snow at the second cow path.

After several runs, we figured out how to stay on the door to the bottom. The bare metal and wet snow on the door sled made us so cold that I finally had to give up. Our clothes were soaked, but we had discovered a great way to slide down the hills of our pasture. The old refrigerator door stayed in the pasture year round as a reminder of the fun times we had in the snow.

The Dam

One of the current events that all the farmers and people who lived along the Republican River talked about was the construction of a huge dam that would span the Republican Valley. The dam, which was to be named Harlan County Dam, was being built to prevent the disastrous floods that occurred on the Republican River every decade or so. Also, the dam would provide irrigation to the farmers downstream along the Republican River all the way into Kansas. It would also become a recreational area for all the people in south central Nebraska.

The dam was to be built just downstream from the old town of Republican City, which was located about thirty-eight miles west of Red Cloud. The problem was that the little town of Republican City was located right along the Republican River. When the dam was completed and filled, Republican City would be underwater.

As the dam was constructed, the town had to be moved to higher ground. This was pretty exciting stuff. It wasn't everyday an entire town had to move!

One spring weekend, our family decided to drive to the new Harlan County Dam site and see what was happening. When we arrived at the visitor's site, we could see what looked like hundreds of bulldozers, graders, and earth blades shaving the land into a whole new configuration. The dam and flood gates were all but completed. A road actually traveled across the top of the dam and along earthen dikes.

Graders were shaping the slope of the dikes along each side of the dam gates. We drove to the new Republican City town site to see where the new town would rise up out of the fields on the north side of the river valley. We had a picnic near what was to become the second largest body of water in Nebraska.

In June of 1952, the dam was dedicated, and water was already flooding the Republican Valley up river from the dam. All along the Republican Valley to the east, a vast network of irrigation canals and ditches were built to change dry land farming into irrigation farming forever. From what we knew at the time, our farm would remain a dry land farm. We knew the irrigation ditches would never reach our farm. (We could not imagine giant, rotating irrigation pivots crawling across the farm land north of the river valley as they are today).

Driving Lessons

My dad took a job working at the Ammunition Depot near Hastings in order to make enough money for our needs. With his daily absence, Mom felt that she needed to rise to the challenge and learn how to drive to the mailbox and back.

She and I figured that between what I knew and what she knew, she could learn to drive. I had driven the tractors. And I had watched my dad drive the car. I knew how to start the car, but could not reach the clutch, brake, and throttle.

We got the car started. I showed Mom where reverse was, and we talked about how the clutch had to be pushed in when the gear shift was moved. After killing the engine several times, the car lurched backward.

When we were ready to go forward, Mom pushed in the clutch while I showed her where first gear was. We agreed to leave the car in first gear for a while. She killed the engine several times. Finally, in lurching motion, the car was rolling forward in first gear.

She wanted to stop at the end of the driveway, but she pushed the brake in without pushing in the clutch. Again the car jumped and died. We talked about the need to use the clutch for starting and stopping. She restarted the car and turned right as she let the clutch out in first gear.

We drove all the way to the mailbox in first gear so Mom could concentrate on steering the car. It was hard to concentrate because of the racing sound of the engine. At the mailbox we needed to stop, back up, turn toward home and get the car going in first gear. We made the trip home just fine, but I am not sure the car's transmission felt just fine. The challenge for the second trip to the mailbox was to shift gears with the clutch while the car was moving. Despite the grinding of the gears, we succeeded. Soon Mom went to the mailbox, driving on her own.

The End of the Farm

The farm began to fail as the 1953 fall season progressed. I became aware that the crops were not abundant. I heard more discussions between my parents about the difficulty of making ends meet with the unprofitable farm. Our equipment was old and worn out.

In December a man came to the farm, my dad showed him around, he took notes and left. Dad and Mom lined up all the farm machinery and straightened up the buildings. On December 31, 1953, cars and trucks came to the farm. The man who had visited a few weeks before started moving with the crowd from building to building, auctioning off each piece of equipment and livestock that we had. In the garage beside the windmill, some ladies sold hot drinks, sandwiches, and pastries to the people who had come to buy our things. It was wet, muddy, and bitter cold that day. The next week the farm equipment and livestock were moved away from our farm. Likewise, that week we loaded our household goods and moved into Red Cloud.

chapter twelve
a new beginning in red cloud

We moved into a small house on Seward Street between 1st and 2nd Avenue. I do not really remember much about that house. The one thing I remember clearly is that for the first time in our family's life, we had an indoor bathroom. That was a great improvement over the one-holer outhouse on the farm. We had toilet paper to use instead of the catalog pages we used in the outhouse. With all the houses around, we had lots of kids to play with also.

New School

I was enrolled into the second half of the fourth grade class at Lincoln Elementary School. My sister Barb went to eighth grade and my brother went to tenth grade at Washington School. Going from a country school of less than a dozen kids in eight grades to a class of thirty-four students in one grade was, to say the least, overwhelming.

Mrs. Vance was my fourth grade teacher. Our class was on the top floor on the southwest side of the school building. The third, fifth, and sixth grade classes were also on the top floor of the school. The younger grades were on the middle floor. The total attendance at Lincoln Elementary School must have been about 230 plus students. That was amazing to me!

Mrs. Vance gave me my books and had me sit at a desk on the west wall near the windows. School was hard for me because I had not studied the courses from the first part of the school year. Starting school in the middle of the year was difficult. I was quiet and timid.

As I got to know the other students, I realized that some lived on farms like I had. Others had only lived in town and knew little about life on a farm. Of course, I knew little about living in town. The popular kids hung together in groups. Some kids seemed to have no friends. The kids whose parents owned businesses downtown were always dressed the nicest. Some kids liked sports activities. Some kids were in Cub Scouts and Girl Scouts. Some kids were really smart and always had their school assignments done. Some always raised their hand when the teacher wanted participation from the students. And one or two kids were always being disciplined for acting up in class.

As I got to know the kids in my neighborhood, they were the kids who I became friends with in school, even though they may have been in an older or younger class. We rode our bikes back and forth to school, or we oftentimes walked together to and from school. School was only about five blocks from my house.

It did not take long for me to realize that I could not read or spell as well as most of the other students. I could not spell the word phonetics, nor did I know its meaning or how to use it. Also, arithmetic was hard because I was not taught to the same level in the one room school as the students in town. I was a C student in fourth grade.

I was intrigued by the stories that Mrs. Vance told about her travels. I particularly remember her trip to the southern part of the United States. She showed us the moss that grew on live oak trees. The moss hung down 4 or 5 feet. She showed us things that she collected from foreign countries. As I think back, geography was the most interesting subject, because I had never traveled more than 50 miles from Red Cloud.

At noon during recess time, I was surprised by the activities. There were high swings and really high slides. There were monkey bars, teeter-totters, and merry-go-rounds. I quickly learned from the other kids that we could climb up the fire escape slide from the ground to the top floor of the school. The fire escape was a gigantic tube maybe 36 inches in diameter that clung to the side of the school like a caterpillar hangs onto the bark of a tree. Once turned around and situated, we could slide down at great speed to the bottom and shoot out on our feet running. If one was really good at sliding, a piece of wax paper made us go even faster. The teachers did not like us to go onto the fire escape. Sometimes to avoid teachers we would visit the super slide on Saturdays. Some kids played in the sports activities like basketball or touch football.

As spring came around, the games turned to jacks and marbles played on or near the sidewalk around the edge of the school building. I did not have jacks or marbles so I just watched others play those games. On warm sunny days, the box elder bugs flew all around the warm sidewalk and brick walls of the school where the students played. I did not recall box elder bugs being abundant on the farm. I suppose the chickens ate them.

New Routines

Living in town was really different. For one thing, we had no chores to do.

I had time to ride my bike to Grandma and Grandpa Hager's house. I even rode over to the north side of town to visit Grandpa Hesman. He seemed really lonely and appreciated the company. Sometimes the neighbor kids organized games in the evening like Hide-and-Go-Seek or Kick-the-Can. The park was only a block or so from our house. We rode our bikes on the sidewalks and played on the playground equipment. I realized riding bikes on sidewalks was a lot better than dirt roads: no more Texas Sand Burs. Some kids had comic books, so we went to their house to read the comic books. Before living in town, the only times I saw comic books was when we were in town for Sale Day or to sell our eggs and cream. I went into the Rexall Drugs to see the comic books at the magazine rack.

Mom did not drive in town, so if she needed something, she walked to downtown. Of course, she did not have the morning and evening farm chores to do, so she had a lot of time on her hands. Dad was gone a lot because he continued to work near Hastings at the Ammunition Depot. He left early and got home late. My sister Barb and brother Ken got involved with activities in High School. Ken really liked track. As spring came on, he spent most of his time over at the track field.

Another New House

Just when I thought we were settled in the house on Seward Street, we moved to a house across the street from Grandpa Hesman. Our new address was 905 N. Webster Street also, Highway 281. The house had two bedrooms upstairs, one was for Barb. Ken and I shared the other. The imaginary line down the center of the bed was defended more than ever by my big brother. It was clear to me that the alligators had relocated to the usual spot under my bed. I continued to make sure no body parts hung over the edge of my bed.

Downstairs were two enclosed porches: one on the front, which was never used, and one on the backside, which was always used. In the front of the house was a bedroom and living room. In the back of the house was a dining room, kitchen, and bathroom. There were a couple storage sheds and a garage that leaned badly to the east. The side street was graveled. Our yard, where cars were parked, was dirt that turned to sticky mud after a rain.

New Jobs

My dad decided he wanted to drive trucks for a living instead of working at the Ammunition Depot. He drove across the country for Mayflower Van Lines. He was gone for many weeks. In that job, not only did he have to drive the truck, he had to load the huge trailer with the mover's belongings and then unload the truck at the new location. There was no rest because he had to drive to the next location. And so it went; my dad was dragging.

When he finally returned home, he got a job driving livestock trucks for the stockyards south of town. At least the cows, pigs, and sheep walked on and off the truck on their own. Ken took a job at the Palace Bakery downtown. Mom got a job cleaning houses. Barb found new friends. I got a paper route for *The Grit* weekly paper.

A New Paper Route

The first thing I did was buy saddle baskets for the back wheel of my bike. I was taught my route and how to collect money once a month. To my knowledge, I was the only person who sold and delivered *The Grit* paper in Red Cloud at that time. The papers were delivered to the Post Office each Saturday morning. My job started early every Saturday morning when I went to the dock door in back of the Post Office. A postal worker let me in to collect the papers. It was exciting, because not only had I seen the front entrance of this impressive building with all the amazing murals, but also now, I was one of the few people who was allowed to see how large the building was in the back and how the mail was processed. I saw Postal workers sticking mail into the open backs of the hundreds of boxes on the wall. Also, I was able to see the mail bags and big mail carts being filled and prepared to go all over the world. The postal workers were always nice to me as I waited for them to give me my bundle of *Grit* papers.

I was paid twenty cents for each issue by my customers, and then I paid The Grit Paper Company ten cents per paper. I had about twenty customers at addresses all over town. The deliveries were made on Saturdays: rain, snow, or shine year-round. Sometimes my parents took me on my route, but most of the time I was on my own. I collected the cost of the papers once a month from my customers. I used a punch card for each customer so I knew the number of papers for which each customer owed. My problem was catching my customers at home so they could pay up. I had to send the money I owed The Grit Paper Company once a month. I had to be careful to have enough money from my customers to pay The Grit Paper Company on time. I learned a lot about the importance of cash flow and creative avoidance from my customers on paying their monthly bill.

I remember a lot of the homes around town to which I delivered. Two places stand out in my memory.

One was interesting, and the other was a challenge. The interesting house was a yellow mansion on the west side of town on Highway 136. When I delivered the paper, I simply put the paper on the side porch. However, when I collected once a month, I was invited inside to wait until the family member found the right change. I could not help but gaze at the interior with all the shelves of books, beautiful woodwork, and large lights hanging from the ceilings. Never had I been in such a magnificent home. And little did I know, this magnificent home would become a Historical Museum for all of Webster County.

The challenging delivery location was west on Highway 136. The home was the last house at that time on the north side of Highway 136. The challenge I faced each week came from the house next door. They had a St. Bernard that loved to chase bicycles; at least he loved to chase my bicycle. I had to pass the beautiful house, where the St. Bernard lived, as I rode my bicycle on Highway 136. When I got near the house with the St. Bernard, I rode quietly, but picked up speed as fast as I could go. The St. Bernard always came from behind the house about the time I was half the distance across the front of their yard. When the St. Bernard intersected me with my bike, it was barking and growling. I swung over to the opposite side of the bike and coasted the rest of the way. I often yelled at the dog, "Go home!" That was the easy part.

Of course, the dog knew I had to return across the same route on the road in front of his yard. I tried to watch the dog while I was on the backside of my customer's house. When I thought the timing was right, I rode from the driveway onto the highway as fast as I could go. If he was all the way in the backyard, I could, most of the time, outrun the dog while yelling for him to "Go home!" The huge dog never bit me, and he never wrecked my bike. He just seemed to enjoy vigorously intimidating me. I kept the paper route for about three years.

A New Car

Another big change, after we moved into town, was that my parents traded in the old '37 Chevy for a '47 Commander Studebaker (marked with an * in the picture). The all black Studebaker was nice and clean with lots of room in the back. It had a radio! Compared to the small trunk of the Chevy, the Studebaker's trunk was gigantic. It seemed like a bed could fit in that trunk. The back seat doors opened forward like my Grandpa Hesman's '47 Plymouth. I was always very careful to keep the back doors locked when we were driving.

While Dad was out of town driving the truck, Mom needed to get her driver's license. A driver's license enabled her to drive to the homes in town that she cleaned each week.

One Saturday, Mom and I went out to the Studebaker to see if we could start it and learn to drive a car with a column shifter and clutch. We learned that the starter button was engaged when the clutch was pushed all the way to the floor. Mom practiced shifting on the steering column. We figured we were ready.

We backed out of the driveway onto the street. We went up the hill away from Webster Street, so she stalled the engine several times. Eventually, mom got the hang of the column shifter. From there we drove around the countryside until Mom felt she was ready to drive with the official of the Department of Motor Vehicles. Together, we studied the driver's manual. She passed her driving test the first time. Mom always praised me for teaching her how to drive. I was eleven-years-old at the time.

A New Vaccine

One of the current events I noticed in the newspaper and the movie newsreels was something called polio. We saw people with their heads sticking out of big tanks, iron lungs, which helped them to breathe. Little children and adults were shown with steel braces on their legs, using crutches to get around. The news sounded alarming, as if there was some sort of worldwide disease that all of us might get sooner or later. There were lots of stories of famous people, even our past President Roosevelt, who talked about the dreaded disease. Rumors circulated about a vaccine that was being made that everyone would have to take. The vaccine did not use just one shot, but several shots!

Not only was I worried that I might get polio, but also, I was worried about getting those shots. I knew I was between a rock and a hard place. I did not want polio and end up in one of those iron lungs; nor did I want lots of shots in my who-knows-where.

I remembered the penicillin shots I got when my tonsils were taken out. I was taken into the little room with white painted cabinets full of little bottles and packages. There was a lamp on a tall stand and high bed that I had to sit on. The nurse, whom I thought was not very compassionate, held the little penicillin bottle upside down, stuck an unnecessarily big needle in the rubber tip of the bottle, flicked the little bottle with her finger as the fluid entered the syringe, pulled the needle out of the bottle, and squirted a little of the fluid back out to remove air bubbles. By this point in the process, fear had set in. Next, it was time to pull down my pants, bend over (which was embarrassing), get a cold moist wipe from the nurse on the spot that was in danger, and then "wham" came the needle, in went the fluid with my butt stinging all the way. The needle was pulled out, and the damaged spot was once again wiped with the cold alcohol. After each shot the nurse said, "Now that wasn't so bad." I always thought, "Not for you." I pulled up my pants and got out of the room, light-headed and unaware of my surroundings. But I always remembered the incident with clarity.

Finally one day, my mom said I was going to get my polio shot. Everyone seemed nervous because the vaccine itself might cause polio. Getting the vaccination was determined to be a lower risk than the risk of being exposed to the disease of polio. On that first visit to Dr. Bennett, I received my first polio shot. But, the shot was not given in the butt. The nurse had me take off my shirt. As I knew she would, she took the little bottle, needle, and syringe and prepared her syringe. Then she took the cold wet cotton and wiped my arm. As she impaled my arm with what looked to me like a big nail, I flinched as the needle was stuck into the muscle. She said, "Oh, you should not have jerked your arm." She pushed the fluid into my muscle and then withdrew the needle. I withstood the pain. When she was done, I walked out of the doctor's office in a fog. I wanted no more of that. I went straight to our car.

In a little while, a lady informed the doctor's receptionist that a little boy was outside lying in the snow next to a car. My parents went outside and found me face down in the snow in a dead faint. When I got my follow-up polio shots, I tried not to flinch as the needle sank into my flesh. I learned to go only outside to the big porch and sit on the porch chair. Then I put my head down between my legs; I avoided passing out this way. To this day, I tell the nurse that I need to lie down to take shots or have any blood drawn. I ask the nurse for the smallest needle. I lie flat until I know I won't faint, and then I sit up.

Best of Friends

During the first couple of years in town, my best friend was my cousin Ronnie.

His home was three blocks up the street to the east. We rode our bikes everywhere. We regularly checked in on our Grandma and Grandpa Hager at their house. Grandpa Hager visited the South Pool Hall on most Sale Days so he could have a beer or two with his friends. Ronnie and I caught him there and stayed a few minutes to visit. A few times we dropped into the Auction Barn and watched cows get auctioned off. We swung by the car dealers to see the new cars.

For spending money, we stocked shelves for Mr. Pierce occasionally. He was the owner of a small grocery next to Dr. Obert's office and across the alley from the telephone office. Also, Mr. Pierce ran the concessions at the Red Cloud football and basketball games. Ronnie and I worked the crowds selling the concession products for Mr. Pierce.

Ronnie and I had die cast metal toy trucks. When we brought our fleet together out in our backyard we imagined we owned a large trucking company. Together we had some good times. There was no doubt in Ronnie's mind that he would become a truck driver. All too soon Ronnie's family moved to McCook, Nebraska. Ronnie's father became a long haul trucker and eventually so did Ronnie. I was never sure what I wanted to do when I grew up.

A New School Year

Through the summer before the fifth grade, I met many of the neighbor kids around the location of our new house. Our house was only a block from the high school. But, our house was fourteen blocks from the elementary school. That did not bother me too much, though, because I was used to traveling a lot farther on my paper route. When school started, I tended to take different routes to school. Midwest towns are generally laid out in compass directions. Red Cloud is no different. It was very easy to avoid getting lost. Sometimes I went through downtown. Sometimes I went by the jail and cut across the courthouse property. There was a network of sidewalks that created a small shortcut. Sometimes, I went straight west then dropped south out by our Lutheran church and then passed in front of the Studebaker garage on my way into the schoolyard.

In the fifth grade, the school teacher was Mrs. Davis. School was easier because I was more familiar with my surroundings. Plus, I had more acquaintances from which to make friends. I got Cs and Bs for grades. One of my classmates who was in Cub Scouts invited me to join Scouts so I gave it a try. Our den met in a home near the edge of what is now the new hospital property. I moved up through the Cub Scout ranks and became a Den Chief. This was the first time I had ever provided leadership for anyone. It felt right.

New Technology

While the fifth grade class experience was not remarkable, one thing that changed the stories and conversations amongst the kids at school was television. More and more families were buying a television. It was easy to tell who was fortunate to have a television because those houses had antennas on the roof. One day I noticed an antenna on my Grandpa's house, so I hurried across the street to his house; inside the parlor was a television.

I lay on the floor that evening and watched this new marvel. The screen was almost round. The picture was quite snowy. But it was exciting to see shows and news in black and white pictures from faraway places. Every night I went across the street to watch Grandpa's TV. He liked watching the news, weather, boxing, and baseball the most. I breathed in a lot of cigar smoke that winter.

Also, I got to know my Grandpa a lot more than I ever had before the TV arrived. Sometimes other members of my family and I were at his house to watch television. Many times it was just he and I in that dimly lit parlor. We did not talk much, but I think he liked the company. He had a special rocking chair that he sat in. He was tall, large, round-faced, and bald and always wore suspenders. He looked like an old, overweight Mr. Clean. When he was ready to smoke, he took a cigar out of his shirt pocket, cut the cigar in half and put one half back into his shirt pocket. The cigar wrapping was pulled off the cigar that he was about to smoke and discarded. The fresh cigar was moistened by his tongue. Then he chewed a small piece off the uncut end and spit the small end piece into his spittoon next to his rocking chair. He moistened the cigar one more time. Next, he struck a match and held it under the cut end of the cigar. He inhaled and drew the flame into the cigar until it showed a red-hot tip. Then, he shook the fire out of the match and put it into his standing ashtray. He drew in long, contented inhalations of smoke until he was sure the cigar would stay lit. Then he sat back, puffed on his cigar, and watched television with me.

At our house, we did not get a television until the following year. Everyone in the family sat in the living room watching the game shows, sports, news, and weather. My spot in the room was on the floor with my elbows propping my hands up under my chin. It was always coolest on the floor during warm evenings, and no one wanted to take my place. Everyone talked about the *Ed Sullivan Show* on Sunday nights. Elvis the trucker had just landed on the stage of Rock and Roll. Other Rock and Roll singers were quick to follow once they got their first shot on the *Ed Sullivan Show*.

Each morning before school, we started the day off with Dave Garroway on the *Today Show*. We got our quick fix of news, sports, and weather. When I got home from school, the television was on while my sister watched *American Bandstand*. Also, shows like *The Flintstones*, *Howdy Doody*, *Mickey Mouse Club*, and *Superman* were on in the afternoon. At supper time we watched *The Huntley-Brinkley Report*; they switched back and forth from New York to Washington D.C. while telling us about the Cold War with Russia: whether there might be nuclear war in the future; missiles that Russia had built and how many the United States had built; civil rights demonstrations and sit-in; disasters all around the world; and what the Government was doing from day to day. After supper, we watched shows like *$64,000 Question*, *The Honeymooners*, *I Love Lucy*, *Gunsmoke*, *Roy Rogers*, *The Adventures of Robin Hood*, *Dragnet*, *Wyatt Earp*, *This is Your Life*, and *The Dinah Shore Show*. Once a week, Edward R. Murrow on *Person To Person* showed us how famous people lived. Also, he showed us how to smoke. This new media of television, it seemed to me, taught us more about the world than our school did.

New Travels

My dad drove four different livestock trucks over the eight years he drove trucks out of Red Cloud. When he was in town, he spent his time at the stockyards near the railroad tracks south of Red Cloud. He drove livestock mostly to Omaha, but went many times to places like Denver, Salt Lake City,

Oklahoma City, Fort Worth, Wichita, and Chicago. Mom went with Dad a number of times. I went to some local places and once to Omaha. Sitting up high in that big truck made me feel tall and strong. I felt that the little cars whizzing around us better be careful because we could certainly win in a fender bender. The engine noise made talking difficult. I enjoyed looking into the mirror and watching the black smoke rise out of the exhaust stack as my dad shifted gears.

At home, Dad told many stories of near misses where other drivers failed to understand the need for wide turns and long stopping distances. Ice and snow were a nightmare for a trucker, as the trailer tried to jackknife when the brakes were applied.

Stock trucks were pretty dirty with manure. When cattle were hauled, the cows stood on the truck trailer floor. When sheep or pigs were hauled, a second floor of wood planking was added into the trailer. The driver generally loaded his own truck. When the trailer had two floors, loading required going into the trailer with the livestock; a pretty dirty job especially when an animal on the upper deck relieved itself at the time the driver was in the trailer on the lower deck. Goats were used to lead sheep into the trailer. Sheep would not go up the ramp into the truck without being led. Many livestock yards had trained goats to lead the sheep up the ramp into the truck. The goat went all the way to the front of the trailer then circled along the edge of the trailer back to the tail gate and on out of the trailer. At that point the tailgate of the trailer was dropped closed. In hot weather, all the livestock became vulnerable to dropping from the heat. Once they were down, it was almost impossible for them to get back up onto their feet. Pigs were especially vulnerable. At truck stops, the pigs were sprayed down with a water hose to give them relief from the heat.

Truckers always liked to tell the funny experiences that they had on the highway. One story that Dad told was when he had a load of cattle on a hot day. Cows sometimes got the runs from riding in the truck and from the heat. Dad could tell a car was following too close to the back of his truck. A convertible car with a man and woman in it pulled out into the passing lane. About half-way along side of the trailer, a cow decided to relieve itself. Its rear was against the side of the trailer. The boards on a livestock truck had spaces between them for keeping the livestock as cool as possible. Out went the poop and into the convertible it landed. The two occupants in the convertible were devastated and dirty. On up the highway they sped with their arms swinging in the air. I am sure they stopped at the nearest service station to get the car, and themselves, cleaned up.

A New Phobia

One day my dad had to go to the dentist. For some reason, I tagged along with him. He had several cavities that needed filled.

Our family went to Dr. Aukes. Dad and I climbed the long stairs to his office. At the top of the stairs, the landing turned back toward the front of the bank building. Dr. Aukes' examination room had a window that looked out over The main street. There were the usual dentist's cabinets, a folding back dental chair, a pull-down, round overhead light, a drill that hung on the end of a crane-like arm with its pulleys and belts that made it operate. Beside the dental chair was the ceramic fountain into which everyone got to spit blood and saliva after the doctor had picked, drilled, and chipped away in their mouths.

Instead of waiting in the waiting area, I walked into the room where Dad got his teeth repaired. Dr. Aukes did not seem to care.

I stood at the side of the fountain to watch. Dad sat in the chair looking the way that a dog looks when it knows it is about to get an unwanted bath.

Dr. Aukes got out his tools and put them onto a tray in front of Dad. The tools were shiny chrome. Some tools had points that were straight; some were curled forward and around; some had flat little chisels on the end; and one had a little round mirror. Also, on the tray was a large round shiny syringe that had a plunger with a circular loop on top into which the Doctor's thumb fit. On the other end was a short but fat, tapered needle.

Dr. Aukes pitched Dad backward and peered into his mouth.

Next, he grabbed the oversized syringe and stuck it into Dad's mouth. I stepped forward to see the action. The sharp needle sunk right into Dad's gum next to a tooth. The doctor pushed in some Novocain as Dad squirmed. Out the needle came, and it went right back into the gum on the other side of the tooth; in went more Novocain. Dad had three teeth to be filled. So the doctor kept sticking that big needle into Dad's gums again and again. Dad squirmed less and less as the Novocain started to deaden his mouth.

I was shocked. I do not remember what happened next to Dad, but I went back into the waiting room. I was sweaty and light-headed. After a while, Dad came out of the room looking slightly pale. He could not talk because his lips and mouth were still numb.

After the doctor talked to Dad about his next visit, we trudged down the long steep stairs. All day long I thought about those shots. Each time Dad slobbered on himself while complaining about his numb mouth, it brought back the memories of what I had witnessed.

I decided the Novocain shots were worse than getting your teeth drilled. To this day, I have had many teeth drilled and two crowns put on without the use of Novocain shots. Each dentist I have seen attempts to convince me to accept the Novocain, but I always grab the arms on the chair and say, "Just drill."

New Car Envy

In those days, my bicycle was really my means of keeping myself busy. Often, I went around to all the car dealers to see the new model cars, sometimes, I was with my friends. We could not help but want to see the new cars because television made them look so good and the people inside them looked so happy.

The Chevy dealer was across from the Standard Service Station. The Ford Dealer was across from the lumber yard. The Ely's Chrysler/Plymouth dealer was across from Dr. Obert's office. The dealers did not seem to mind our visits and our excitement; I guess they knew we were future car owners. The changes in cars were amazing. The designs went from tall and rounded to lower and wider shapes. Fins on the back fenders started showing up as well.

The Corvette and Thunderbird were introduced by Chevy and Ford respectively; these were cars we could not even imagine, and yet, they were real. The huge and powerful Chrysler 300 arrived in Red Cloud; the 300 horsepower engine was called the HEMI. This car was the first of the muscle cars. Ford invented plastic tops through which the sky could be seen. Ford was the first to introduce the hard top convertible. Of all the cars from the 50s era, Chevy's classic 1957 Belair two-door hardtop has been my favorite.

Automatic transmissions were becoming the norm. Power steering and power brakes were soon added into the standard options to improve the driving experience. I knew these things because I got the new model year brochures at the dealer's showroom. I read them and dreamed about one day owning and driving them. I sat in front of our house, named the cars and their model year as they traveled north and south on Webster Street/Highway 281.

Even though my dad owned a '47 Studebaker, and I appreciated its longer lower look, I really never liked it. I think Dad and Mom were able to get the Studebaker because few people wanted one. My parents got a good price. In the early 1950s, the Studebaker design morphed into what looked to me like a cornpicker with its three points on the front end. The best time we had with our Studebaker was when we went on a vacation to the Black Hills of South Dakota.

New Sights to See

After loading up the Studebaker, we drove to Grand Island and headed west toward the Sand Hills of Nebraska. We turned north and visited some people (to this day I do not know who they were) in Chadron, where we stayed overnight. I remember the huge farmer's breakfast served.

From there we drove into the south side of the Black Hills National Forest. We stopped at Needles Rocks, where it was hard to drive through. Next, we went to Mount Rushmore. It was almost impossible to comprehend the height and size of the carvings. I was awed by the fact that someone had thought up a way to make those giant faces on the side of a mountain. At the visitor's center, we looked at the construction pictures and were amazed. These were the first mountains that I had seen.

Along the way, we stopped for a picnic lunch. After lunch, I disappeared to climb a very high bluff. When I got to the top, I called down to my family. They were shocked and urged me to back away from the edge and come back down, which I did. I was the center of an angry conversation for quite a ways up the highway. We ended our Black Hills trip by exploring the gold mining town and western shops of Deadwood, South Dakota.

I remember looking out the car window as we dropped down into the deepest, craggiest gulch I had ever seen. The narrow street had weather worn shops, saloons, and hotels that created mystery and intrigue. Little did I know, Grandpa Hesman's childhood stories as a small boy about Wild Bill Hickok's Wild West Shows and the sharp shooting of Calamity Jane in those shows, would come to life for me right there in Deadwood. In 1876, Wild Bill Hickcok was shot dead in one of Deadwood's saloons. Wild Bill was buried in the Deadwood Cemetery. He was later moved to the Mt. Mariah Cemetery. Calamity Jane was buried right beside him. We drove to the cemetery to see their graves. I was convinced that Deadwood was one wild town back in those gold mining days.

Deadwood was my favorite place to visit on our Black Hills vacation. I do not remember anything about the drive back home. I guess I must have slept a lot. The vacation was really only a couple days long, but I talked about the sights I had seen for years afterward.

A New Way of Fishing

One weekend the car was packed with fishing and cooking gear. My dad, my brother Ken, and I drove to a fishing spot along the river. At that site, Grandpa Hesman, Uncle Fred, and some cousins were converging for a family fishing event. One of the men started a campfire. Some other men prepared the bait: chicken entrails, corn kernels, worms, tadpoles, cut up frogs and toads, and anything else that the men thought catfish would eat. Then a long heavy throw line was uncoiled. There were many shorter lines with hooks attached hanging from the long line. The bait was attached to the hooks. The throw line was tied to a small tree on the shore of the river. On the other end, a heavy pointed mower sickle guard was tied. The sickle guard was pointed and heavy, making it a good anchor for the throw line. The men set several fishing lines out in the river.

When the lines were set, the men and boys gathered around the fire to talk. The men smoked and enjoyed some refreshments that the kids could not have. Instead, the kids got Kool-Aid, and roasted hot dogs. As the evening progressed, the mosquitoes always found targets for their kamikaze lifestyle. After a while, the men pulled the throw line onto the riverbank. Wriggling angry fish of all kinds were caught on the hooks attached to the throw line. The fish that were large enough and considered to be edible fish were removed from the hooks and put onto strings floating in the water. The other fish were released or used as bait for the next line going out. The fish were pan-sized up to arm's length. Most were catfish.

Grandpa knew about catfish. He was like a catfish magician compared to the rest of us. He demonstrated his magic by getting into the water along overhangs from the bank. He reached into the water under the overhang and slowly felt around with his hands. When he felt a fish, he slid his hand along the fish until he found the mouth. As the catfish breathed through his mouth and gills, Grandpa slid his hand into the fish's mouth and pulled up hard with a strong grip. Water flew everywhere as he brought the fish up to its untimely demise. Most of the time Grandpa's fish were bigger than the hook-caught fish! I don't think my dad or uncle tried hand fishing.

When it was late enough in the evening, all the lines were coiled and put away. The fire was covered with sand. All the fishing and cooking gear was put back into the cars. Everyone was celebrating the catch and telling the tales of the big fish that were caught. We said our goodbyes and went home. We ate fried fish that whole week from the bounty of our fishing expedition.

A New Grade in School

In the sixth grade, my teacher was Mrs. Grice. I was still a C and B student. I did my homework, but was not the greatest with participation. The best event of the school year was when our class did its operetta on stage at the State Theater. I had no memorizing to do. The play was Jack and the Beanstalk. One of the scenes had a cow called Juliana. I was the rear end of Juliana. Being from a farm, I figured I could handle being the south end of a cow going north.

We had to make our costumes. My acting partner and I made a papier-mache black and white cow head. A white sheet with painted black spots was attached to the head. We painted our jeans white with black spots. A tail was attached to the sheet on the rear. As we did our part in the play, I swished the tail and raised my leg to scratch Juliana's front leg. The crowd loved the humor of that scene. The play went well. I don't think we got grades out of that effort, though. For making the crowd laugh, the cow should have gotten an A+.

A New Job

In 1956, my paper route was not keeping me with adequate spending money. I needed some more money. So in addition to delivering *The Grit*, I worked as a pinsetter in the new bowling alley. The bowling alley was just south of the IGA Grocery Store on the east side of The main street. In order to work there, I needed to get my Social Security Card. Unfortunately, this also meant that the government now knew that I was a taxable citizen.

A lot of my friends worked at the bowling alley during the evenings and weekends. We got to know each other pretty well as we worked in the back of that bowling alley. We were paid by the lines set. If there were no customers, it was not worth our time. But we had to take the bad times with the good. League nights were the best nights to work. In the back of the bowling alley, there were three to four foot high walls behind each of the four bowling alleys. A two by ten inch board was nailed across the top of the wall. That is where the pinsetter sat while the bowling balls were thrown. The back wall had a heavy rubber pad into which the ball crashed before falling into the pit with the pins.

At the back end of each bowling lane, there were walls on each side. Above the pins, were mechanical pin setting machines. The mechanical pin setting machines were held in an up position by a locking handle bar, so that the machines did not to get in the way of the bowling balls hitting the upright bowling pins. This configuration created a pit into which the pins and ball were contained after a player threw the ball.

The thrown ball crashed through the pins. Pins flew all over that pit. Most of the time, they were contained between the side walls and back wall. Sometimes pins flew into another pit or across the back wall. It was important to keep an eye out for rebel pins headed for pinsetter's head!

After the ball landed, the pinsetter jumped off the wall into the pit with the ball and downed pins. The ball was lifted onto a return ramp that carried it back to the front of the bowling alley and onto the ball rack. The pins that were knocked over were gathered up and placed into the respective pin rack pockets. The pins rested in the rack pockets on their side until they were ready to be reset.

When the second ball was thrown, the process was repeated. Sometimes the bowler got ahead of the pin-setter and threw the ball when we were still in the pit. They could see us pinsetters picking up the pins. We could hear the ball drop and make its rolling sound as it traveled toward the remaining pins and us. We yelled in disgust at the impatient bowler. After the second ball, the pin rack had to be lowered. The pinsetter unlocked the handlebar and set the loaded rack down onto the alley surface. All the pins tipped onto their bottoms and stood upright. The spring-loaded pin rack lifted back into its raised position for the next player. Each pinsetter took care of two alleys. We worked from about 5PM to 10PM. The pinsetters could go home when their alleys were empty at closing. We took memories of the job home with us in the form of bruises from those rebel pins flying up and hitting their mark. Most of us younger pinsetters rode our bikes home in the dark. If it was a weeknight, we still had to be at school early the next morning.

New Changes for Ken

My brother played on the baseball team in the spring and summer for several years. Every now and then my parents drove to the ball park to watch Ken play ball, so I rode along. Most of the time I went to the ball field on my bike. The ball field was located on the east edge of town, down in a low level area near Highway 136 behind a farmer union type of service station. As I recall, there were no charges for watching the games. Towns around Red Cloud came to play. Sometimes I got to be a bat boy. But most of the time, I chased foul balls. When a foul ball went over the fence or behind the bleachers, a number of kids chased the ball. I think we got ten cents for a returned ball. To me, chasing foul balls was more exciting than watching the game.

My brother graduated from high school in '56. He went into the National Guard. Then, he bought a nice '52 Ford. He studied telegraphy, which used Morse Code and a magnetic clapper device that could send and receive the Morse Code over telephone wires. He soon moved to Guernsey, Wyoming where he worked for the railroad sending Morse Code before there was short wave radio systems.

Having my brother leave was not in my list of objectives, but no longer was there an imaginary line down the middle of the bed. Also, I got the room to myself, except for the pesky alligators living under my bed.

A New Time for Mother and Son

My dad was still gone most of the time, driving the truck. My sister was gone a lot, spending time with her friends. Sometimes Mom and I walked downtown to see a movie. It was only a four block walk. We often stopped at the library along our way.

She had gotten a job at a restaurant washing dishes, so at times I walked her to the restaurant. On our way, she talked about things she wanted me to know. I talked about things I wanted her to know. Sometimes we had pretty good talks. One evening after a movie, we were walking home in the early darkness. We noticed the sky was dancing in colors of blues, greens, yellows, and reds. The colors swirled all around overhead. It was eerie and beautiful. We were amazed by the intensity of the color and speed of the swirls. The event was something I had never seen before. Mom thought the show was the Northern Lights. By the time we got home, the light show had disappeared. That was a good time walking to and from town with Mom.

Giant Combines

One of my favorite memories of the midsummer was watching the harvest crews head up Highway 281 in front of my house toward South and North Dakota. Truck after truck was loaded with huge combines chained to their backs: green, red, and a few were orange. The large combine driver wheels hung halfway over each side of the trucks and were pushed tight against the cabs of the trucks. The rear steering wheels hung over the ends of the trucks as if the dangling wheels were trying to reach the road. Each truck towed a trailer with the long combine cutter head and rotors that fit to the front of the combine body. Amongst the combine-laden trucks were other grain trucks loaded with supplies to keep both the harvesters and machines going day and night. Some smaller trucks towed well-worn trailer houses which were the mobile homes of the harvesters and families.

These giant machines and crews traveled in caravans from the south and moved north as the grain matured and became ready for harvest. As the summer progressed, the harvesting crews and machines made their way well up into Canada before the harvest season was over. If one could look from an airplane, they must have looked like giant insects eating all the vegetation on the great fields of grain across the midland of America.

Watching the parade of green, red, and orange monsters of the highway caused me to wonder who those men were. Did they have their wives and children with them? Was it fun to drive the giant machines? Where did they stay at night? The combine people were the prairie adventurers of my time.

A New Extravaganza in Town

Late in the summer, the circus came to town. The circus tents were set up on the ball field. Many of us kids watched the tents being pulled up the long poles by the elephants. Every circus worker knew what their job was and how to do it just right. We kids even went in amongst the workers and animals to help. I think we did not really help though. The animals seemed to know what their jobs were as well. Everything came out of the trucks in a certain order. It was like a new village appeared in Red Cloud in just a few hours.

Once it was set up, there was a matinee and an evening show. All kinds of circus toys, balloons, pinwheels and snacks could be bought, if you had any money. It was an amazing show.

In a couple days the circus was gone. The ball field was again empty.

The only other real circus I had seen was the one time when we went to the Shriner's Circus in Hastings, Nebraska. That show had three rings and lots of fancy costumes. There were more toys than a young mind could comprehend. At that circus, I bought a live salamander that changed colors. How cool is that for a kid? I brought it home. A string was tied around its neck with a safety pin tied to the other end. The string was its leash.

The next day there was a spot of sunshine on the sofa on the porch. I thought the salamander would enjoy some sun. But, I didn't want to lose him, so I pinned the little reptile to the sofa. I went outside for a while. When I got back, the pinned leash was empty. Our cat was sitting near that spot licking its lips. I was really mad.

The "New" Mower

One day as I was riding my bike around the neighborhood, I noticed a broken-down mower near the alley in a backyard. I asked the owner if he needed the mower any more. He said he did not. I rode home and asked my dad to take the Studebaker over to the man's house to pick up the used mower. I told him that I wanted to mow lawns to earn more money. He said okay, and we did. My dad was not too sure that it was worth taking home. But I convinced him that it was worth it, so we brought the beat up mower home.

My big, three-wheeled mower was a sorry looking site, but it was *my* mower. I had never owned something so valuable that was mine alone. In front, there was one wheel that rotated for steering. That wheel was broken. I rode my bike to the Coast-to-Coast Hardware store for a replacement wheel. I found one and rode home to replace the old wheel. Dad was pretty good at keeping things running because that was what farmers needed to do when their equipment broke down. He brought the engine back to life and got the mower running pretty well. We sharpened the blade. Now, I was ready to be a young entrepreneur in the mowing business.

The motor required a rope to be wound around the flywheel on top of the engine. When the rope was wound, a strong fast pull on the rope handle was needed. Because the rotating front wheel allowed the mower to turn toward me as I pulled the rope, I blocked the mower with one foot on the deck of the mower. After a few tries, I was able to get the mower running. Dad had a gas can with some gas, so I mowed our lawn as my first trial run.

What I soon learned was that with the rotating front wheel, our slanted front yard caused the mower to turn sharply down the slope to the curb and onto the street. I realized that I had a pretty significant problem. I was still too small to keep the mower straight on a side hill. It was too heavy to push straight up the slope from the road. Most of my potential customers up and down our side of Webster Street had sloped lawns to the road.

My solution was to step to the backside of the mower deck placing one hand on the yoke of the mower handlebar and the other hand on the back side of the handlebar. I leaned over and pushed on the yoke, while holding the mower straight as it traveled on the slope of the lawn. Keeping the mower straight and pushing it forward took all the strength I had. On the flat areas, the mower worked well and was really powerful.

After successfully completing one lawn, I went around the neighborhood and made deals with about a dozen customers for repeat mowing. For other customers, I just watched the grass grow on un-mowed lawns and then asked the homeowners if they wanted their yard mowed. If the lawn was average size, I charged a dollar; for a large lawn, I charged two dollars. That spring and summer I was in the flush with cash.

I was putting a lot of hours on the mower. I learned how to change the oil and adjust the carburetor to keep it running well. After a while, the engine was hard to keep running. One Saturday morning my dad was teaching me how to change the spark plug and points. We did the repairs and were giving the engine a trial run. I came around the side of the mower and stepped under the rotating mower. I heard a loud grinding sound and the mower stopped. I looked down at my foot and saw the front end of my tennis shoe gone. I started hopping on one foot holding the other bleeding foot with one hand. Around the yard I went, hopping and yelling. When Dad finally caught me, he helped me hobble onto the back porch. By then my mom heard all the commotion and met us on the porch. I set down on the couch while my parents got my shoe off. It looked bad, so I yelled more.

After the bleeding slowed down and the wound was washed, we could see a number of horizontal cuts into my big toe. The blade of the mower did not lop off parts of my toe, but instead sliced into the end of my toe. My parents determined that the blade of the mower had not hit the bone. I was so lucky not to have had my toes cut off! My mom wrapped gauze around and over my toe. I rested my foot on a chair. My toe throbbed like someone was squeezing the toe with a pair of pliers.

The front porch was where I stayed for the next couple of days. Fortunately, I had been wearing my new oversized tennis shoes. The rubber at the end of the tennis shoe took most of the blade's wrath. I counted about twenty cuts through the tennis shoe, but my toe only took about five slices. Of course, I was out of the mowing business for a week or so. I learned a lifelong lesson about allowing the mower near my feet and wearing heavy shoes while moving. I mowed lawns with that mower for a couple of seasons.

New Creatures

Every once in a while in an effort to find adventure, my friends and I rode our bikes north on Highway 281. The town power plant and a bridge across Crooked Creek were just outside of town. We hid our bikes under the bridge. Sitting under the bridge was fun because cars and trucks made a loud noise over our heads as they crossed the bridge. The brushy, shaded creek was a great place to explore and wade along the creek bed. There were clear, sandy spots of shallow, fast running water, and in some places the creek had some dark, deep wading holes. Along the sides there were pools of water from when the water was higher after a rain.

In those pools there were little round black tadpoles with long flat tails propelling them through the water. Depending on the stage of their growth, they might only have tails. At other times, we could see a leg growing on each side of the tail. After that, the front legs appeared, the back legs were fully developed, and the tail disappeared. Later on, they took on the shape of a little frog. In some pools it seemed like there were hundreds of the little creatures. Sometimes we took some home for fish bait. If we carefully tended to the water and fed the tadpoles, they grew into little frogs. Unfortunately, they always disappeared because they could climb out of the container and hop away.

On one trip to the creek we were wading in the deep side pools of water. After a while, we noticed blood running down our legs. Slimy black squiggly leeches were attaching themselves to us. At first, we were scared to leave them on us. Later, we kind of observed that they got larger as they sucked our blood. When we pulled them off there was a little sting, and a little blood ran down our wet legs. When we went into the main creek, we washed off. We noticed that the leeches tended to be in the still side pools along the creek. On later trips to the creeks we watched for the little black leeches. If we saw them, we stayed out of those pools of water.

We noticed other interesting creatures also. We could see one to three-inch long fish darting around in the shallow clear water. Sometimes we even spotted crawfish scooting along backwards just as they saw us. There never were many crawfish in that creek that we could see, so it was a special thrill to spy one.

Going home, every once in a while, we could see that the big doors on the side of the power plant were open. We carefully observed the fenced in property to see if anyone was around. If not, at a fast pace, we rode our bikes through the gate, down into the power plant area, and near to the open doors. We could see the large equipment running noisily inside. The whole building seemed to make a groaning sound. Steam rose up and out of the big pipes on the roof of the building. We never took too long circling in front of the open door on our bikes. We always got out of there fast, because we did not want to get caught.

A New Best Friend

In 1956, I got my own dog. We had always had family dogs since I could remember, but this time one of the dogs was mine! Our all-black family dog had puppies; one of the pups was all white with big, black spots. I named her Toni.

She was the cutest, wiggliest little puppy. She grew up to be covered with curls. We went everywhere together. I could not take her on my bike, but I found a baby stroller frame. I secured a piece of canvas to create a nest-like seat in the stroller. When she needed to get out of the house, I walked her in the stroller. People thought it was stupid or cute. I did not care. My sister hated to have her friends see me pushing Toni in the stroller. When I figured out that this activity embarrassed her in front of her friends, I made sure I was out walking the dog when they came to our house. This was one of my sources of enjoyment.

As the little brother, I was pretty hard on my sister. When she and her friends teased me, I dished the sassiness right back. When they got the best of me, I called them all "chicken dabs." That was the worst cuss word I was allowed to say. When I used those words, it always seemed to get a rise out of my parents, but they did not get so upset that it was risky for me. Being from the farm I could have chosen "cow manure," "pig slop," or "horse pucky." It seemed to me that "chicken dab" was the correct level of bad language though. My sister's teenage friends got a kick out of my retaliation. While my sister joined the fun, I think it made her mad. She has many times reminded me how I unnecessarily and all too often used the words "chicken dab."

chapter thirteen
the middle school years

At the end of the summer, big changes were about to occur. Not only had my brother left to work in Wyoming, but also I was headed to junior high school in the Washington School building.

The seventh and eighth grade classes met on the end of the high school building. The Washington School was only a block away from my house. Now, I could walk to school if I wanted.

School was really different in town. There were no playgrounds or recess breaks. The big high school students were all around the school. As I recall, we junior high kids did not dare to look an upper class high school student right in the eye. The freshmen were underdogs, but it seemed like we seventh graders were subterranean dogs.

Our teachers advised us to stick to the end of the building nearest our classrooms. We had to spend more time on the lower floor also, because the bathrooms, locker rooms, and gymnasium were only accessible by a long hallway down through the middle of the building. Of course, being in the same building, we seventh graders bumped into the big guys quite a lot.

Mrs. Amack was my teacher. She was a very nice teacher and taught all the required courses. Science was added to our curriculum in a big way. I thought the science course made school much more interesting. I was doing better in my scholastic achievement; I was getting B's most often now.

Scout Troop 100

By now, I had been in the Boy Scouts for a year. We were Scout Troop 100. Our neck scarves were Red and Gold, just like our Red Cloud Warrior colors. We met downtown in a basement on the east side of Webster Street in the area of the South Pool Hall. Mr. Eldred, who owned the Alis-Chalmers Tractor Store on the north end of town, was our Scout Master. Sometimes we met in the Eldred's basement. I was well into my merit badge program. As I completed each merit badge project, I moved onto the next badge.

The first merit badge was first aid. We had to learn the various bandages and slings to be applied for injuries and broken bones. We learned how to help a person who was not breathing or who was overcome by heat. We studied the Boy Scout First Aid manual.

Another merit badge was animal husbandry. My project was to shadow a veterinarian. The town veterinarian, Dr. Raspberry, let me ride with him to a farm that had a sick cow. I could not believe what I saw! The veterinarian took a walnut-sized tablet in his hand and put his arm into that cow's backside clear up to his shoulder. Right then and there I knew I would never be a veterinarian!

The next day I was invited to watch a surgery on a little dog. The dog got a shot which put her to sleep. The dog was laid on her back and her belly was shaved. Dr. Raspberry took his scalpel and cut right down the middle of that little dog's belly. I got weak. I was glad I did not have to help because it was all I could do to keep from throwing up and fainting. Finally, after doing some things inside the little dog the opening was sewn shut. I tried to appear like that was no big deal. However, I am sure Dr. Raspberry knew better. I was happy when I left and got some fresh air. I had to write a report about my veterinarian visit.

Another merit badge I worked on was for cycling. For the cycling merit badge, we had to demonstrate that we could repair our bicycle and fix flat tires. We also had to disassemble and lubricate our bicycles. From my farm experience, I was well equipped to work on my bike. We took several ten-mile trips around Red Cloud as well.

One of the ten-mile trips was to Inavale; we circled around the small village and returned home. The other was almost to Guide Rock. We had heard of the Zebulan Pike gun pits on the river road just west of Guide Rock. So we took a route to the spot where we could walk out to the top of a hill. There, we could actually see shallow dips in the grass where Pike's gun pits were. From the high spot, we looked out across the river bottomland where a thousand Pawnee Indians once lived in their huts.

In 1806, Lt. Zebulon Pike of the US Army and a small party of soldiers, an interpreter, and a doctor came out of Kansas up to the Republican Pawnee Community located on the Republican River between the locations of what are now Guide Rock and Red Cloud. Pike and his men stayed a couple extra weeks observing and negotiating with the Pawnee Leaders to change their allegiance from the Spanish to the United States. Pike convinced the Pawnees to take the Spanish Flag down and start flying the United States Flag. Pike left the area and continued his expedition through the Southwest.

On our way home, we turned into the property of the Starke Round Barn at Amboy. The Starke Round Barn still stands. It is Nebraska's largest barn. It measures one hundred and thirty feet in diameter with the barn having three levels; the ground floor for livestock, the middle level for farm equipment, and the top level for hay. After a short rest, we rode on back to Red Cloud.

The big trip for our cycling merit badge was fifty miles. A half dozen of us scouts rode our bikes from Red Cloud to Blue Hill. Highway 281 did not have much of a shoulder on which we could ride. When trucks passed, the wind and suction from the trucks was pretty risky for us bikers. Two miles north of town was the dirt road that went east to where I was born. At six miles, the intersection to Cowles reminded me of the many times traveled for the visits to the tiny community that few people knew about. As we rode by the intersection eight miles north of town, I could see the farm on which I had lived. To my knowledge no other family lived on that farm after our family. The farm looked broken down. It was odd for me because my life on that farm seemed like another life that I had lived. Another half mile, I could see the earthen dam where I rode the bulldozer. Several more miles ahead we rode by the empty and deteriorating Tin School House that sat right beside Highway 281. Not long after, we made our way around the fourteen-mile corner north of Red Cloud; I could see my Aunt and Uncle's farm across the fields to the northwest. We traveled east to the next long turn from Route 4. Our final leg on the trip north took us to the town of Blue Hill. We rode around Blue Hill enough that we knew we would achieve the fifty-mile ride. We ate our lunch at the park near the train station. In the early afternoon, we began our ride back to Red Cloud. I was somewhat surprised at how long the ride was, and that we accomplished the ride without any problems. The next day I could hardly walk, and the saddle soreness was something that only a cowboy or biker could understand.

On occasion our troop went camping locally in areas near town. A couple times I was able to go to some larger scout camps. Tin-foil dinners were the main food source on our campouts. At home, we used a square section of tin foil and placed a piece of butter in the center. Next, we added diced potatoes, carrots, and some chopped onions then finally added a generous hamburger patty to the top. The final flourish was sprinkling salt and pepper on top. Depending on one's taste, other ingredients could be thrown into the mix. The tin foil was carefully folded over the contents to prevent leaks. A second square of tin foil was folded over the first silver package. The tin-foil dinner feast was stored for later in our backpacks.

At camp the fire was built up into a large bed of coals. When only the red-hot coals remained, we carefully placed our tin-foil dinners onto the coals. Soon the savory meals could be heard sizzling in the coals. Each scout had to time the cooking of his meal. In about twenty to thirty minutes the hot bundle of foil was lifted out and placed on a log, stump, or rock. The tin-foil was cut open with one's multi-bladed Scout knife, the steam rose out of the cut foil. The aroma was unmistakably the foretaste of a woodland feast. Even if the potatoes were not completely cooked or the meat was a little dry, the anticipation of the reward was all that mattered.

This dinner had its nightmare scenarios as well: they all involved tin-foil packages with a pinhole or rip. If the foil package was carelessly folded or packed in one's backpack, the foil ended up with a perforation. Or, worst of all, if the sizzling bundle was poked while it cooked on the hot coals, the contents charred instead of roasting. Everyone could tell who had a leak in his dinner package because the faint burnt smell was unmistakable. When the scout knife cut that bundle open, the burnt smell filled the campsite. The scorched food was picked through in hopes of something edible remaining, because the other scouts knew it was a long wait until the next meal.

If we stayed overnight, we did the usual things like start a fire. A location to relieve oneself had to be prepared. Tents were pitched. Sometimes in the evenings we hiked out from the main camp. We sang songs like *99 Bottles of Beer on the Wall* as we hiked along. We did projects that helped us earn merit badges. We told ghost stories around the campfire. We scouts got to know each other pretty well on these trips. We learned a lot of wise advice from our Scout Masters.

The scout program created balance in the choices that young boys need to make as they move through adolescence into their teen years. The scouts were important associates and friends around town and in school. I came to know some of the scout leaders and scout supporters who were town officials and business owners. They provided good role models for us boys to emulate. They opened doors for scouts needing guidance and jobs in the local community. The Scout Oath and Laws became bedrock values guiding me as I made choices and struggled through my formative years. When I left the Boy Scouts, I had attained Star Rank. There is no doubt that my exposure to the scout program was an invaluable building block and facet of the character I developed.

Barb Meets a Boy

My sister started dating a young man from Hastings named Bob Reinke. He was nice and fun to be around. More important, he owned a yellow, '51 convertible Mercury. It was lowered and had an extended rear bumper for a spare tire cover. That was some car! Every once in a while, I got to ride in that car; I sat up tall so everyone could see me. I am sure I looked pretty cool in that car.

In October, my sister Barbara married Bob at our house. They moved to Bandon, Oregon to work in a lumber mill.

Finally, I had the run of the house. I was the only kid! That felt good. It was pretty easy for Mom and I to decide which programs to watch on television. No more *American Bandstand* in the afternoon!

Bob and Barb's move to Oregon did not work out well. As a result, my new brother-in-law enlisted in the Air Force and went to boot camp in January 1957. Barb returned home. Of course, as one would expect, we all had to make adjustments. By now the beautiful Mercury was gone and Barb was driving a white '55 Ford. Nice, but not exciting. As my brother-in-law went to several bases for his training, sometimes Barb was able to go with him to the location. But, most of the time, she was home with us.

Football in Nebraska

The seventh grade was the beginning of my sports career. I went out for the junior high football team. I must admit early on, I do not mind hard work, but I cannot stand too much pain. I will let you know right now, I was never the Red Cloud sports hero.

The coach decided I was best suited to play right guard. We practiced under the tall pine trees east of the High School gymnasium. Our scrimmages were rough and tough. Every once in a while a nearby town junior high football team came to play against us. We football players walked across town to the high school football field feeling optimistic and empowered. There, we had afternoon games with our competitors. If we won, we walked back to the locker room with lots of hooting and hollering about how good we were. If we lost, we walked quietly, wondering what had gone wrong. Respectively, our showers were loud and rambunctious or meek and quiet.

Our coaches did the best they could to make little boys into future high school football jocks. There were no protective cups for us guys!

Road Trip to Arizona

In June, 1957, my brother-in-law was assigned to the Air Force Base in Tucson, Arizona. My sister needed to move to Tucson to be with him. Bob could not come home to get her. My dad had to stay on his job driving the truck. Mom had her job and did not feel she could drive that far away from town. It was decided I would go with Barb to Arizona. After school was out, we loaded the car. She had some clothes, a television, and enough other things to fill her '55 Ford. We said our goodbyes to Mom and Dad and headed to Arizona.

Between teaching Mom how to drive the Chevy and the Studebaker, and my interest in cars, I knew how to drive my sister's Ford. Barb and I switched off driving. I was thirteen at the time. We went south through Kansas and across the Oklahoma panhandle to Amarillo, Texas. We turned west on Route 66 to Albuquerque, New Mexico.

As we drove across New Mexico, we were in pitch-black darkness on a winding road in rain and heavy fog. We kept driving slowly, looking out the window at the white line beside the car. Finally, the fog cleared, and we were left with rain. Late in the night Barb was sleeping and I was driving. Of course I was unfamiliar with the road; I had only been out of Nebraska once on our trip to the Black Hills. My experience was minimal, to say the least. I saw a sign that said to turn right. I did. Off the road we went at 55 miles an hour down a small incline into a gravel yard along the highway. I hit the brakes. When we got stopped, the television was pretty much on Barb's head. After this event, Barb was completely awake. We got back onto the highway and traveled on to Holbrook, Arizona.

As we studied the map, the route from Holbrook to Tucson looked shorter than through Flagstaff to Phoenix on down to Tucson. We knew the road from Holbrook had some sections of mountainous roads, but it was mid June; surely any snow would be gone. When we got about halfway, we hit a snowstorm on a narrow, winding gravel road. We discussed turning back, but continued on ahead. We were both scared for our safety; we feared getting stuck or sliding off the road. There were almost no other cars. After awhile the road started dropping down from the highest point, and the snow quit. We sighed with relief. Later in the day we made it to Tucson.

Before I left Tucson, Barb and I drove out to the Old Tucson Mission. The day was bright and sunny. We drove through the arid landscape where cactus grew fifteen to twenty feet high. Sagebrush roamed everywhere the wind blew. There were lots of rock formations big and small. I had never seen such an odd, but beautiful landscape. As we were driving along the gravel road, a skinny grayish/brown bird jumped out along our car. We knew it was not a quail or grouse. It started running ahead and alongside our car. He was racing our car for what seemed like a couple minutes. Suddenly, he jumped back into the sagebrush and was quickly camouflaged. We guessed it must have been a roadrunner. The Tucson Mission was very interesting to see, but at that time it was in disrepair.

The next day we went to the Greyhound Bus station. We bought a ticket back to Nebraska for me. I did a lot of sleeping on the bus. There was not much else to do. We drove into the night, stopping at the many bus stops along the way. At the Denver bus stop, I was told I could go no further because there was some kind of work stoppage in the Midwest. I called my parents with the bad news. We agreed that I would sit at the station until they found another way to get me home. I told the bus officials my plan. After a while, they gave me a ticket to Cheyenne, Wyoming. At Cheyenne, I was to change bus lines and go on into Grand Island, Nebraska, which I did. My parents picked me up at the Grand Island bus station. After that trip, I could say I had *really* been out of Nebraska.

Summer Break

The summer of 1957 was hot as usual in our little town. I resumed my lawn mowing business. Plus, I was still working part time at the bowling alley. I gave up *The Grit* paper route and said good-bye to that Saint Bernard.

I spent most of everyday at the Red Cloud swimming pool. The pool was full of kids from mid-morning to the early evening. I learned to swim and dive pretty well. The Sugar and Spice Drive-in operated beside the swimming pool and was a popular hangout for the teenagers around town. Because the swimming pool was at the south end of the park, those of us on bikes hung around the park as well.

One of my poorer judgments that summer was to begin smoking as a thirteen-year-old. Most of the male members of my family smoked (not my brother), so it seemed quite appropriate that I would start experimenting with this vice. Those of us who were sneaking smokes did so in out-of-sight places. It was not difficult to buy cigarettes from legal-age teenagers. Of course, my clothes smelled like smoke, so my parents confronted me. They were disappointed, but said I should not sneak around to smoke; instead, I could smoke at home. Smoking was pretty much an off-and-on thing for me because of sports. I also did not want to smell like smoke at school. I stopped altogether midway through high school, because of sports activities.

My parents realized that I had worn out my old bike finally, so for my fourteenth birthday, they gave me a new bike. It was a classic. It had fenders, a light on the front fender, a tank between the two bars between the seat and handlebars. The tires had white side walls. The front fork was spring loaded. And there was a rack on the back over the fender. That bike was like a Chrysler Imperial compared to a Henry Jay. I only added two items to that amazing bike: steering knobs on each corner of the handlebars.

By the end of the summer, the Air Force reassigned my brother-in-law to another location, so my sister returned home again. My parents decided it was time, before school started, to take a short trip to Guernsey, Wyoming to visit my brother, Ken.

The Guernsey area is located on the route of the Oregon Trail. There are many landmarks to see, such as the deep wagon ruts cut into the rocks between Guernsey and Fort Laramie. Also, Fort Laramie was the site where several major Indian and US Governmental treaties were negotiated and signed. The Fort was a major resupply point for the Oregon Trail pioneers.

In Guernsey, one of the places we visited was the Guernsey

Reservoir. It was the end of the summer, so the lake water was quite warm. We found a small cove to park near the water. Ken, Barb, and I decided to swim in the lake. Near our swimming spot was a small island. Ken swam to the island. Barb went next. Part way across she started to flounder. She disappeared a couple times. Then, she did not come up. I dove in and swam to where she disappeared. I dove down into the water and finally felt her thrashing around down below. To avoid getting caught by her panic, I went deeper, came up under her and pushed her back to the surface. By then my brother was nearby and held her up at the surface. When I got my breath back, Ken and I pulled Barb back to the bank. My parents watched the whole event, feeling helpless; neither Dad nor Mom knew how to swim. We were all thankful that a tragedy had not occurred.

That night we camped at a covered picnic area beside the lake. Ken went back to town to his apartment. Barb slept in her sleeping bag on one of the picnic tables. I slept in my sleeping bag on another picnic table. Mom and Dad slept in the car. In the night, Barb heard some sounds nearby. She woke all of us up hollering about something eating Jim. I responded with surprise as I scampered out of my bedding and jumped up and down on the picnic table. I did not feel like anything was eating me! Relaxing in happiness that I was not being eaten, we looked around the picnic area to see what disturbed Barb. We found partially eaten chicken bones taken from the garbage can. We guessed 'coons had been feasting on the chicken bones, but we were never sure. We all finished the night sleeping in the car.

The next day we met up with my brother and said our good-byes. The trip was short, but had certainly been eventful.

A short while later my brother met his future wife from Wheatland, Wyoming, which was south of Guernsey. My parents and I went to the wedding in Wheatland. Because telegraphy (Morse Code Communication) was being phased out, my brother and sister-in-law moved to Coos Bay, Oregon where he went to work in a paper mill. As fate would have it, they traveled nearly the same route as the pioneers on the Oregon Trail.

The Space Race Begins

The eighth grade was more of the same in terms of English, math, spelling, and history. Beulah Fayle was our teacher. At least as eighth graders, we were now in a position to point out how low the seventh graders were in the pecking order of the Washington School society. The girls in class stood taller than most boys, but we were beginning to show signs of maturity. Our testosterone was kicking in, which meant we were getting stronger, taller, and manlike.

For me, and probably many people, the most outrageous current event of the fall was Sputnik 1. The television, radio, and the *Red Cloud Chief* newspaper reported on the cold war between Russia and the USA. Month after month, onerous news articles about the two countries developing their ability to launch missiles and warheads around the world were in the media. We were in a missile and nuclear race. Suddenly in October of 1957, the news alert of the times was that Russia beat the USA to a successful satellite launch. We saw pictures on TV and in newspapers of Sputnik 1, which I thought looked like a silver ball with four antennas sticking out of it. We could even hear recordings of Sputnik 1's transformer going beep, beep, beep, as it orbited over the USA.

We eighth graders had a lot of discussions in class about what this meant to the USA and its citizens. Our science classes started taking on a whole new importance. I remember hearing on the radio in my room all the speculation about the meaning of the Russians getting into space before the United States. The general fear was that if they could get a satellite in orbit, they could get a bomb to the USA. If a teenager's blood pressure could go up, I am sure mine did! I was concerned.

In November, the Russians did it again. They successfully sent up an 1100-pound Sputnik II with a dog in it! After a few days, the dog died. I was shocked and mad. I have always loved dogs. I thought, "Who did those Russians think they were, to kill a dog up in space?" I could hardly get enough news about all the happenings.

Finally, in January of 1958, the USA launched a successful missile carrying a heavy satellite into space. I thought it was about time for us to catch up. Now the tables were turned. Little did we know what a space race Sputnik started between Russia and the USA.

Another New Job

In the early spring, I asked Marvin Jones, who owned a farm near town, whether he could give me a job. He was starting the planting season and was setting up irrigation on some of his fields near town. He gave me a job setting irrigation tubes in a newly planted corn field. He taught me how to lay out all the tubes along an irrigation ditch and to pump the tubes with my hands to create the flow of water through the tubes. The water in the irrigation ditch came from the Harlan County Dam some forty miles away. A series of canals fed water into the many irrigation ditches all along the farm lands east of the dam. One of those irrigation ditches traveled along the edge of Mr. Jones' cornfield.

The aluminum irrigation tubes were about four feet long and about an inch in diameter. The tubes were bent into an arch at one end. To create the flow of water from the ditch to the row in which water was to travel, the tube was covered with one hand and the arched end was thrust into the irrigation ditch with a pumping action motion. The water was pushed into the tube. When the water pressure squirted water out of the covered end of the tube, the tube was carefully and quickly laid into the row without losing the suction that had been created. Water flowed through the tube and down the rows of new plants. When all the tubes in the field were set and flowing, my job was finished for the day. I worked on Saturday morning and sometimes on Sunday mornings. I was thankful to Mr. Jones for my new job.

A Public Declaration

In May, 1958, the culmination of my Catechism studies at Zion Lutheran Church occurred with my Confirmation. Confirmation in the Lutheran Church is a big deal. All the Bible studies, memorization of the Lutheran Liturgy and certain Bible verses meant I could become a member of the Lutheran Church and take Communion with the rest of the congregation. More importantly, it was a public declaration that I believed in the Lord Jesus Christ as my Savior. This service was important to me and provided an important foundation for my Christian belief in the years to come. And, I might add, my teenage years would challenge my faith in my Lord.

Summer Work for Mr. Jones

When summer came around, I was given a full-time job on Mr. Jones' farm east of town. Our neighbor, Ernie Warner, worked for Mr. Jones as a farm hand. He took me to the fields with him. Ernie and his family lived in a house with a white picket fence, catty-cornered across the intersection from our house. Ernie was a mentor for me as I learned what was expected that summer. I pretty much worked in the hay fields of Mr. Jones' farm. Ernie showed me how to run the Alis-Chalmer tractors and equipment. I learned to cut alfalfa and rake it into rows for bailing. Ernie operated the bailer. Then, he and I picked the bales up with a tractor and low bed hay trailer. Once we loaded the trailer, we hauled the load to the spot where the bails were stacked for sale or for use during the following winter to feed Mr. Jones' cattle. We did this for three or four cuttings of hay that summer. I found working the hay to be really hard. The heat in the summer sun on those fields was intense. The bales were heavy. As I grew stronger and developed more muscles, the work got easier.

The other work that was expected of me was to change the irrigation sprinkling system in the growth stage of the alfalfa season. Long four-inch aluminum sections of pipe had to be moved one by one across the fields each morning and evening. Each pipe had twist locks to fit and hold the pipes together and a sprinkler head in the middle of each section of pipe. The mainline pipe from the pump engine was six- inch pipe. As the pipe was relocated across the field from the pump, new sections of six-inch pipe had to be added to the mainline pipe. Once I moved and adjusted the pipe, I started the pump for that round of sprinkling water on the new growth of hay. The huge pump drew its water from one of the irrigation canals that ran across Mr. Jones' farmland.

Not only did Ernie Warner work as a farm hand, he ran the projectors at Mr. Jones' State Theater located in the Besse Auditorium in Red Cloud.

Working at the State Theater

The Besse Building was built in 1920. Over 800 opera chairs seated attendees who went to the operas presented on the grand stage. In 1925, the State Theater was opened as a theater to utilize the new technology of motion pictures.

Mr. Jones decided to train me to run the movie projectors at his theater. I was to be a relief projectionist for Ernie Warner. Through the summer of 1958, Ernie taught me how to: run the two projectors, splice film, make up the previews film for coming attractions, turn on all the switches for theater lighting, turn on and test the sound system, open and close the theater building, and do the interim janitorial services required between movie showings.

This job was by far my most complicated job to date. The projection room was a small room located at the back of the theater near the ceiling. Outside the projector room was a large unused room that had once been used for important community events. The projectors in the 50s and 60s were about six feet high. A full eighteen-inch reel was placed into the feed reel position. About eight feet of leader film was inserted into all the film gear/gates that ran through the projector section, then through the audio section of the projector and onto an empty reel spool at the bottom of the projector. When loaded, the projector ran for a short moment to insure the film was tracking properly through all the gears.

Next, the arc lamp housing was opened. The lamp was about the size of two five gallon buckets placed end to end. The lamp had a stovepipe going out the roof of the building. In this device, a feed system ran two sticks of arc rods together with about a quarter inch gap. When electricity was applied, the rods created a bright arch, like a continuous welding rod arc. A lot of heat was created by the arc from the rods. In the end of the lamp was a highly polished concave mirror that concentrated the light through the projector and film onto the theater screen.

The projectionist had to determine which reels were to be run on which projector at any given time. During a movie, the first projector and light was turned on and set to run. When it was time for the movie to begin, the light gate was opened and the projector started at the right time for the movie to be seen and heard by the movie guests sitting in the theater. When the running reel was about empty, the second projector arc lamp was started. At the end of a reel of film, a warning flashed on the screen that the public did not tend to notice. That flash was the signal for the projectionist to start running the second projector. In about ten seconds, two circles flashed at the corner of the screen. In one second, another circle on the corner of the screen flashed. At that time the light gate was opened so that the second projector began projecting the movie onto the screen. The change in projectors, if done right, was not noticed by the untrained eye of the spectators watching the movie.

The projectionist went to the first projector, which was no longer showing the film on the screen, and shut both the projector and lamp down. The reel at the bottom of the projector, which held all the film, was removed from the projector. The empty reel on top was moved to the bottom and the appropriate new, full reel was placed in the top reel housing. The leader from the full reel was fed through the projector then tested for running and the lamp was checked for proper length of arc rods. When done, the projector was ready for showing the next reel of film on the screen when it was time.

While the movie ran, the reversed reel of film that was removed from the projector was put on a re-winder to run the film back on to an empty spool to its correct position for the next showing. Each movie had five or six reels for a complete show. Plus, there was a comic strip movie and the coming attractions film strip that was shown at the beginning of the show. Long epic movies like *Gone with the Wind* might have nine or ten reels of film. It took about twenty minutes for a reel of film to be run through the projector. The projectionist had to make sure the next projector was ready before the other projector ran out.

It was a busy place when things ran well. But when a film broke in the projector, which it did from time to time, the projectionist had to shut the projector down. The theater went dark. The lights in the theater went on. The bad film had to be removed from the projector. The good film was fed through the projector onto another empty reel. When done, the projector and lamp were started and the light gate opened for the show to go on.

As one can imagine, this was not a desired situation. Normally, the people in the theater were quiet at first; but at some point they always started yelling and whistling for the show to resume. For me, that moment was filled with pressure. The projectionist had to have a cool head and a steady hand to get the projector back up and running. While this was going on, the next projector had to be ready to run by the end of the reel that failed. The broken film needed to be re-spliced during the rewinding process. If there were two or more breaks in the film, it became chaotic because the crowd got mad, and it doubled our work in the projection room.

The worst film break I experienced was when the film tore and split the film lengthwise at a sprocket after the projection level and before the audio level. One side of the split film kept running through the audio section of the projector, but the other side of the film was jamming up inside the projector. Nothing appeared wrong on the screen. After a while the picture on the screen started jumping. I opened up the doors on the running projector and wads of torn film fell to the floor. I shut down the projector; the crowd started letting me know they were unhappy. I pulled out the torn film. I had film all over the projector floor. The only thing I could do was rethread the remaining reel into the projector and restart the movie. The reel I removed from the projector had fifty to sixty feet, maybe more, of damaged film wound on it. The other half of the strip of film was mashed and torn on the floor. I cut off the bad section of film and re-spliced the reel when I had time. At the next showing of that film, I am sorry to say, a brief part of that movie was gone forever.

Movies like *Ben Hur*, *Some Like It Hot*, *Sleeping Beauty*, *The Diary of Ann Frank*, and a number of Elvis movies were some of the movies shown in my days as a projectionist. For a while, there were midnight movies shown on Friday nights. The high school crowd from Red Cloud and the other towns around came to see those shows. They were the creepy horror movies of the time like *The Fly*, *Psycho*, *The Tingler*, *Dracula*, *Frankenstein*, and reruns of old movies like *The Mummy* and *The Wolf Man*. *The Blob* was the worst movie for me to run as a projectionist. *The Blob* was an outer space shapeless creature that could slip through cracks and under doors. It ate everything with blood. During that show, I could not help but watch for something sliding in under the door into the dimly lit projection room.

For every activity and movie showing, Mr. Jones and his family opened the building, sold tickets, and made popcorn for that matinee or evening event. If there was something wrong during a movie, like the sound was too low or the movie picture was getting too dark, Mr. Jones pushed a button downstairs that made a buzzer sound in the projection room. The projectionist was expected to correct the problem fast.

After the shows, the projectionist turned janitor. The theater had to be swept. The restrooms had to be cleaned. The women's restroom was typically trashed up more than the men's. I am not sure what the significance of that was. Finally, the trash had to be gathered up and put in the back near the alley back door. If there was a change in movies for the week, new movie posters were put into the glass cases just outside the front doors of the theater.

The State Theater was an interesting building. The building had a lot of sounds that made it kind of spooky. In the stage area, behind the screen, the stored back drop could be seen hanging high in the structure overhead. When the theater was used for school plays, band concerts, or public activities, ropes lifted the movie screen up. A backdrop with the scene of trees and a road disappearing into the far distance was rolled down. For school plays, stage scenes were created just for that play. Each scene backdrop was dropped down at the right time. There were long black side curtains to hide the offstage activities between scenes in the school plays. Many students from all grade levels and years have been on that stage or were busy with activities in the back. Lots of memories were created in that theater.

chapter fourteen
a nebraskan high schooler

It was a relief to move into the upper echelon of life at Washington School, but I was only a freshman. There was still a pecking order. At this time, our life brought additional changes because of family circumstances.

The Move Across the Street

As Grandpa Hesman got older, my mom spent more time helping him with cooking and housekeeping. My grandpa had a stroke and spent some time in the hospital. He recuperated well enough to return home. Grandpa and my parents decided it was time to move into Grandpa's house across the street. Mom would no longer need to do housekeeping in two homes, and Grandpa would have live-in help to meet his needs.

We moved our belongings across the street and started the three generational living arrangements. My parents and Grandpa took the two downstairs bedrooms. I took the larger bedroom upstairs. That room suited me just fine. I got the second television in my room. I could easily keep to myself. Once again, the alligators relocated to their dark spot under my bed. I knew then that I would never outgrow this fear implanted in my psyche. I would never dangle my feet over the edge of my bed in the future. I realized eventually I needed to find a wife who understood my eccentricity.

Mom had her hands full with our move. Dad was still gone through the week, but home a lot on the weekends. I was a teenager with my own agenda.

Grandpa needed a lot of help and had to change some habits, like smoking in the house so much and using the spittoon. The television program schedule was negotiated with Mom. And, with only one bathroom, we developed a schedule for routine use. As the months went by, Grandpa required an increasing amount of personal attention and care.

Mom enjoyed sprucing the house up with new wallpaper and living room furniture. She even bought an exercise machine. The machine was designed in three parts. The middle was a round padded seat with a motor that moved the seat in a circular motion. On the left was a part that made a bench for the upper torso. On the right side was another bench that held the legs and feet. The two benches attached to the middle motorized section. The person was to lie down on the bench with the hips positioned over the middle round seat. There was a heavy sand bag that was put across the hips and thighs. When the motor was turned on, the circular motion moved the hip section of the body around and around. The sand bag created a counter motion on the top of the hips. It was relaxing and kind of fun. I do not think it was good for aerobics or weight loss. It was just an early version of an exercise machine. I do not think Mom spent much time on that crazy machine. My Grandpa's house had become our home.

Freshman Year Begins

In the fall of 1958, our freshman class began. There were many teachers and classrooms. When the bell rang, all the high school students went into the halls of the school to make their way to the next class, restrooms, lockers, or gym. In ten minutes or less, the halls were silent again for the next hour. Of course, the freshmen were the underclass, but it was a different feeling to be in high school. Our class grew to forty-two members because additional students joined us from other junior high schools near Red Cloud. There were new students to meet and get to know.

Some students picked band or sports. Some managed to do it all. I did not take anything special. I had English, geography, science, algebra, physical education, and drivers' education (which was probably a little late in the game). Although I had taught my Mom how to drive and I drove my sister to Arizona,

I thought it was great officially learning how to drive during school hours. It was a joy.

Physical education was not graded; the student got unsatisfactory or satisfactory. I got Satisfactory-minus (S-) the first semester. I thought, "How can a student who hauled bales of hay all summer long, get an S- in PE?" Although I must admit climbing that rope to the ceiling of the gym was not easy. I did play basketball that year as a Guard. My problem was not being able to hit the basket so I was not very helpful to the team. I learned basketball was not the sport for me. I tried band using my brother's clarinet; that instrument just seemed to squeal, plus, I could not figure out how to read those notes. Certainly, I was not going to try out for band using my sister's glockenspiel (bells). The ninth grade was not my finest moment; however, I did get an S for Satisfactory in PE in the second semester.

One of our teachers was Mr. Borowicz. He taught English. He also owned a brand new Volkswagen Beetle. One day he turned the corner off Webster Street and drove in front of the high school building to park his VW Beetle. He went into the school building. A bunch of us students gathered around the car like dogs when they gather around to smell a new dog in the neighborhood. We looked in front, in back, on the sides, underneath, and inside. It actually had four seats in that tiny interior. The motor was in the back not in the front. The motor sounded like a Cushman scooter. It certainly was not an attractive little car. It looked like a rolling, black dung beetle that one sees on cow pies in a pasture.

Mr. Borowicz was an independent thinker and well liked by the students. We kidded him a lot about the little foreign car that did not seem safe on the highway. Only a couple decades before, the world was fighting Germany; now, they wanted us to buy and drive their unattractive little cars. It made no sense to me why someone would drive something other than a Ford, General Motors, or Chrysler. But there it was, a VW Beetle setting there in front of our school. Mr. Borowicz loved his little car and drove it for as long as I was in high school, and probably well beyond.

J.C. Penney Stock Boy

Halfway through the ninth grade I turned fifteen-and-a-half. That meant two things; First, I could get my learner's permit. Second, I needed to earn more money to buy my first car. This was clear motivation for me to get an additional job at the J.C. Penney store as a stock boy. That job taught me that not only did people come in sizes, but also, they came in dimensions, such as A, B, C, and D cups. Or they were petite, small, medium, or large. Or they had narrow, normal, or wide feet. They could be short, regular, or tall. Their neck could be fourteen-and-a-half to eighteen inches around. Their arms could run from thirty-two inches to thirty-eight inches in length. They were either a child, junior, or miss. Heads ranged from six-and-a-quarter to eight inches around. It was my job down in the basement to appropriately mark and price each item that came in the back doors, according to size or dimension.

Every evening or Saturday morning when I arrived, I was greeted with large boxes from all over the world piled behind my work table. I opened each box and found the invoice revealing the contents of the box. Then, I matched the contents with the order. Next, I counted each item by size and dimension. For the next step, I made a pin/label for each item. To make a pin/label, I inserted little letters or numbers into a printing device. Strips of blank pin/labels fed into the printing machine. The item name, code, size, dimension, and price were printed onto pin/labels. The pin/labels were attached to the clothing item in the correct locations. Finally, all the items were hung with their appropriate hangers on racks which were eventually taken to the main floor to be sold.

When each item was sold, the sales clerk pulled the pin/label from the item and included it with the customer's money. The store clerk sent the pin/label and money to a clerk in the balcony area in the back of the store, using a spring-loaded conveyor system and tube. The appropriate change and receipt was returned on the conveyor to the sales clerk. The customer got the receipt, change, and the purchased item in a J.C. Penney sack.

When I was finished with the inventory and labeling process, I stocked the sales counters with appropriate sacks, emptied the trash bins, and oil mopped the old, squeaky hardwood floors. Once a week, I went up into the balcony area in the back of the store to pick up my pay. My pay was always in a little manila envelope with a slip of paper showing the hours paid and the correct amount of cash. J.C. Penney was a great place to work.

The Willa Cather Foundation Moves In

Being the small town that Red Cloud was, any new activity was known by everyone. One activity was the renovation of the old, magnificent Garber Bank Building. The red-stoned building built by Silas Garber was always mysterious to me. It towered above Webster Street on the east side across from Penney's. Its architecture was entirely different than any of the other long, square-shaped buildings along the main thoroughfare. One's imagination could easily make the building into a castle or a haunted dwelling for human beings of the past.

Demolition materials were hauled out of the building by the truckload. While the walls were being restored and refinished, a buddy of mine and I asked if we could go into the tall, complicated building to see what it was like. The rooms in front were relatively small, and the stairs wound around the small rooms all the way to the top. I had never seen such an interesting building.

Some ladies were inside the building, making plans for its future use. They explained that the building would provide a home for the Willa Cather Foundation. The worthy building was to be the beginning of many renovation projects in the coming decades to preserve buildings and sites that were the basis for many of Willa Cather's stories and books.

I remember our family doctor's wife, Mrs. Mildred Bennett, had been to our high school several times. She explained the significance of Willa Cather being a famous author who wrote fictional books and stories about various places and families in and around Red Cloud. Mrs. Bennett explained to us students the plans of the Cather Organization for the promotion and restoration of places that were necessary for the preservation of the history of Willa Cather. Mrs. Bennett's information confirmed some of the stories about Willa Cather I had heard growing up in Red Cloud.

While Willa Cather's history and notoriety was present all around town at the turn of the twentieth century, her importance seemed like no big deal in the 50s and 60s, at least to me. Somehow over the years, living in Red Cloud, I became aware of the unassuming house on 3rd and Cedar where Willa Cather lived as a child. It was a small house with a picket fence around the property. In addition, on Webster Street, the main street in downtown, just adjacent to the State Bank building, was the building in which the Coast-To-Coast Hardware store was located. On that building, the roof peak displayed the words Opera House 1895. In my teenage days, no one could go up the stairs to see the Opera House stage area. Rumors were that the famous author, Willa Cather, had spent a lot of time attending the performances held up there. I knew that she graduated from Red Cloud High School, and that her high school graduation took place on the Opera House stage.

Mrs. Bennett explained in her talks to us students that a movie had been made from Willa Cather's book *A Lost Lady*. The movie premiered in Red Cloud at the Besse Auditorium/Theater, which I thought was neat because I ran the projectors at the theater. Even though Mrs. Bennett spoke so enthusiastically about the famous author Willa Cather, I never decided to read any of Willa Cather's books; nor do I remember any high school assignments/book reports to learn more about her and her stories.

An English Essay Revisited

One of our English assignments in high school *was* to write an essay about a real situation. I decided to ask my Grandpa Hesman to tell me about his life so I could write an essay about him. My essay read as follows:

> Jim Hesman's parents came to the United States in the year of 1871. They came from Czechoslovakia by boat. They boarded a train to Wisconsin. They stayed there four years, 1875, but decided to come to Nebraska. By train they traveled to Sutton and walked from Sutton to their homestead which was located two miles east of Blue Hill. When they found their land, Grandpa's dad walked to Bloomington, Nebraska to get papers for his farm to be. This was in 1876.
>
> In 1877 there was a prairie fire that started where Hastings is now and stopped on the Republican River. They fought it with ditches, one was fifty foot wide and the fire jumped it. It drove right over the top of the Hesman dugout and killed the turkeys and chickens, but the cow was in the dugout.
>
> The next year Indians camped on the Hesman land. They took all of the melons that had been planted that year, but they did not do that without paying. One morning the wagon was missing and it was gone all day. Later on, the wagon was pulled back filled with corn. They did this for thanks. They left that winter, but they returned every year for three years.
>
> In 1881 a new member of the family (arrived), which was my grandpa. In 1888 was the Big

Blizzard. That night Grandpa as a boy went to get
cattle before the storm hit. He was late getting the
cattle and down came the storm. He wandered
through the storm, but he could find no way home.
He heard the pigs squealing, so he followed the
sound. The pigs were in a haystack; he climbed
between the pigs to get warm. After he got warm,
he started out again. By this time there were
people out looking for him. But without help, he
found the house and told his story. When the men
got back, they were short one man. Old man Trine,
and Bill White and Ed White, besides Grandpa's
dad. Bill was the one that was lost. They hunted
that night but it was hopeless. The next morning they found Bill at the schoolhouse a half mile
away. He was alright because there was firewood
for the stove.

That same year Grandpa's mother died
He got married in 1902, to Carrie Nohavec. The
two were unable to have children, so they adopted
quite a few children before they stopped.

1912 was the death year of Grandpa's father.
He worked hard to keep his kids eating. He
adopted my mom and her brother and gave them
a home.

When my grandma died in 1947, it was hard for
him to keep going but he sits in his big rocking
chair smoking cigars and watching television.

    This essay was not well written; I received a B. The greatest
value in this essay is that it captured a moment about a man who
lived at the turn of the century, and it briefly captured his parent's
lives during the later part of the previous century. With Grandpa's deteriorating health, no one would know about the incidents

and family history if it had not been written down for others to read later on. *(See Notes # 1.)*

Spring and Summer in Red Cloud

In the spring of 1959, I was working more and more for Marvin Jones on the farm and at the theater. I learned to feed his cattle, and plow and disc fields for spring planting. Of course there was the spring cutting of alfalfa for hay as well. When school ended, Ernie Warner picked me up and took me to work with him. Ernie purchased a '54 black and white Chevy two door hard top. It was really nice, and he took great care of that car. Every week I saw him washing and cleaning his car across the street from our house. Watching Ernie primp over his car made me more and more anxious to get my first car.

I turned sixteen in August. I passed my driver's test after my birthday, making me an officially licensed driver—finally!

I convinced my dad and mom that I had saved enough money to buy a car and get insurance. For my sixteenth birthday, they agreed I could get my own car! Dad and I went car hunting right away. We found a '49 Ford two-door sedan; it was a faded gray/green color. The shocks were pretty soft. The sides behind the door were rusted through. The radio worked. The seats were pretty dirty. The tires were not that good. The flathead V-8 engine sounded fine. The clutch and transmission seemed to be okay. For $200 it was mine. We brought my "new" car home, and I was as proud as I could be.

As I made money, I bought and installed new shocks. I got better used tires from the Texaco station. I bought and installed new seat covers from the Coast-To-Coast for the front and back seats. I got new spinner hub caps like other cars had in those days. Several wax jobs and a lot of elbow grease helped bring out a little shine. The wax did not help the rusted spots. I put in all new fluids, antifreeze, oil, etc. I filled the gas tank again and again. And so it goes when a car belongs to you. I did not complain. I don't remember riding my bike after I got my car. I do not even remember what happened to the bike I was so proud of owning.

Sophomore Stories

School started; we were sophomores. *Webster's New World Dictionary* from 1960 says a sophomore is "a student in the second year of college or high school." The second definition is "a sophomoric person; know-it-all whose thinking is really immature or foolish." I believe Webster had it about right. Sometimes it is called the tenth grade.

The courses were pretty generic: geometry, world history, English literature, German language and biology. Learning the German language was difficult for me; putting the verb before the subject made no sense to me. Biology was the most interesting class, especially the labs where we dissected lots of pickled things. I took PE again because I decided I did not want to be in any sports programs that year. I had committed to too many evening and weekend jobs. And incorrectly so, I thought I had better things to do.

That year I learned a lot about cars because my Ford needed a lot of attention: radiator, thermostat, clutch, u-joints, tail pipe, muffler, brakes, points and plugs; you name it. I spent a lot of time working on my car at the Texaco Station on the corner across from Lockhart's Malt Shop. So much so, I started trading some of the cost of my parts for doing extra work at the service station. I did things like filling gas tanks, lubricating customers' cars, and fixing customers' flat tires. One of the ways I kept good tires on my car was to use the better used tires from the Texaco customer's cars when they bought new tires.

Cruising was the thing teenage car owners did. Hot rods or clunkers, it made no difference. Gas and tires were made to burn. The Red Cloud main street, Webster Street, was two blocks long. A short cruise meant making a u-turn at the Texaco Station intersection, and cruising back to the intersection at the Post

Office then making a u-turn after the two blocks. A longer cruise would be to make a u-turn at the fire station and cruise to the Sugar and Spice Drive-in for a u-turn or to have some food.

We mostly cruised before and after movies or high school games. On the nights the Inavale roller skating rink was open, we drove the seven miles west to roller skate for the evening. Sometimes we went out of town across the river bridge to the intersection on the south side of the Republican River and returned back to town. If it was late, sometimes we raced our beloved cars across the bridge to the railroad tracks south of town. It did not matter who won or lost; it was the moment that counted.

Escaping Boredom

Some of our activities were meant to prevent Midwest youthful boredom. But one might say, in hindsight, we certainly ran into the category of poor judgment, bordering on stupidity.

In the fall, we went watermelon hunting; that is, we found the hidden watermelon patches and acquired the ripest melons. The watermelon farmers planted the melon fields in the middle of their corn fields in an attempt to keep pesky poachers from the melons. From the road the melon patches were not visible. No one had an airplane to spot the patches from the air; but somehow, the whereabouts of the melon patches were known by the time the fall harvest season rolled around. At night, watermelon raids were planned. When enough melons were gathered from the hidden patches, we kids had a watermelon feast on some quiet country road. There were legends about melon hunters being shot with rock salt by farmers determined to protect their crop. Electric fences running ankle high through the corn fields were installed to surprise unsuspecting melon hunters as well!

In the winter, we went rabbit hunting at night. A couple guys would sit on the front fenders of the car with their .22 rifles at the ready. We drove down snow covered country roads with the car lights shining down the tracks which were made by cars that had already a broken a trail. Inevitably, a rabbit jumped into the lights of the car and ran as fast as he could in the pre-existing car tracks. The rabbits thought they could run faster in the packed track rather than try to run in the soft snow. We tried to outrun them, or we tried to hit them with the .22 rifles. If my memory serves me correctly, the rabbit was smarter than the human. I don't remember hurting a single rabbit. It may have something to do with our next activity.

Kansas Beer Runs

Sometimes we went to Kansas to pick up some 3.2 beer. The 3.2 beer had a lower alcohol content level than Nebraska beer. In those days, buying beer in Kansas was not difficult. It was only twenty miles or so to Lebanon, Kansas. The trip was a nice ride to pick up the forbidden refreshments.

I can recall one snowy night some friends and I had been to Kansas. We had beer and were traveling west toward Riverton. The road was covered with snow; the warm car and loud music felt just right. The beer was plentiful. I was getting warm in the back seat drinking with one of my buddies so I kicked my shoes off. Suddenly, snow started flying up the windshield. Just like slow motion, the car slowly tipped on its side.

When everything stopped, I opened the car door, which was on top, and climbed out. Someone lifted the beer out to me. I hopped down into the grader ditch where the car was lying on its side. I knew we needed not to be caught with beer, when someone, like the police, came by. I was standing in the snow in my socks because my shoes were lost in the car. Up the bank I ran with the beer. I realized, with a shock, that I encountered an electric fence. I had to cross over it, which was not fun, but I made it.

I took the beer quite a ways into the field and ditched it. I returned to the electric fence in my cold wet socks. Over the shocking fence I went. When I got back to the car, the rest of my friends were trying to roll the car back onto its wheels. We got it after several tries. The car started right back up. The only remaining problem was that the car was still in the grader ditch.

We tried to get it out, but could not. We got our coats and shoes, and then hitched a ride back to town. The next day, the owner of the car got his car out of the ditch. I suppose the farmer found the beer we had left behind after the spring thaw.

Four-Wheel Embarrassment

On weekends and holidays from school I often fed Mr. Jones' cattle in the winter. I used Mr. Jones' blue Jeep to haul hay bales out into the frozen fields. The hay was pushed off the truck for the cows to eat during the wintery days. I took Mr. Jones' pickup home so that I could use it several days in a row.

The four-wheel drive Jeep pickup was fun to drive on the muddy roads. A couple friends and I agreed we should take the pickup out for a ride in the mud. We drove out of town to the northwest. The road was very muddy, just what we wanted.

As we started climbing a hill, the pickup started plowing mud. As it did so, the truck moved closer to the edge of the road. We stopped. No matter what I did, the truck kept sliding to the ditch. Finally, both right wheels became mired into the deep muddy ditch. We were really stuck. I thought I was pretty inept to get a four-wheel drive Jeep stuck in the mud.

We walked back to town. Embarrassed as I could be, I went to Mr. Jones and told him what I had done to his Jeep. He looked stern and said he would take care of it. We never mentioned that day of bad judgment, and I never took his pickup home again.

Spring Break Trip and the U-2 Spy Plane

That winter my parents bought a 1953 Desoto four-door sedan. It was all green with lots of chrome and as big as a car could be. Under the hood was a huge Hemi V-8 engine. The car had an automatic transmission with a clutch. If you wanted to use the clutch, the car started off like a standard transmission.

If you wanted to forget the clutch, the car started off like any automatic transmission vehicle. I thought that feature was pretty cool. That meant you could rev up the engine, let the clutch out and spin the rear wheels. The inside was clean as a pin, and the ride was as good as I imagined a limousine would ride.

During spring break, Mom, Dad and I drove the magic carpet, I mean Desoto, to Minot, North Dakota to visit my sister and brother-in-law. My brother-in-law was stationed at the Air Force Base near Minot. I recall several things about that trip.

For miles and miles in North Dakota, we noticed there were large rock piles in all the farmer's fields. Each spring farmers had to pick up rocks from their fields before preparing the fields for planting. The rocks surfaced in the soil during the winter. As the earth repeatedly became frozen and then thawed out, the rocks were pumped to the surface. The rocks were incorporated into the soil during the glacial melting after the Ice Age. As we drove north up Highway 281, we could see that the unearthed rocks were effectively used in all sorts of buildings and foundations.

Somewhere along the long road north, we stopped at a church to use their restrooms. In those days in the rural areas of North Dakota, there were no highway rest stops. Nor were there fast food chains and highway quick stop service stations like we have today. Fortunately, the person at the church was polite in accommodating us. When we left, we said thanks and drove on up the highway. About an hour later, I realized that my wallet was missing. We decided the only thing we could do was go back to the church where we had stopped. Yes, in the restroom toilet stall on the floor was my wallet. I was very relieved to see my wallet and go to the restroom again. We lost about three hours driving time from that little fiasco. My dad was not very happy being the trucker that he was.

When we were in Minot, we toured the city with my sister. It seemed like a pretty large place. There were lots of things to see, as compared to our little town of Red Cloud. We went into stores and ate in a restaurant. As a teenage boy, I was on high alert for girls. It seemed to me that there was an absence of good looking girls. Granted, my number of observations was limited because it was darn cold, and everyone was bundled up. At the time, I had concluded that the snow and freezing weather might have had an unbecoming effect on the girls up north. I left Minot somewhat disappointed. However, having watched a number of Miss America Pageants on television, I have seen plenty of Miss North Dakotans that were not adversely affected by the weather.

The fourth thing I remember about our trip to Minot was that the Air Force Base was on high alert. A high altitude U-2 spy plane from the USA made a flyover near or over the border into Soviet air space. The Russians noticed the air space infraction and were making a lot of aggressive media statements. Of course, the US denied that it was an intentional violation of the Soviet air space. Russian missiles were being readied to prevent repeated atrocities from the USA.

My brother-in-law seemed quite tense about the whole situation. We did not stay too long in Minot because my brother-in-law had to be at the Air Base doing his job as a mechanic on the large Air Force planes.

As it turned out, on May 1st a U-2 plane was shot down by the Russians which started an embarrassing denial of the facts by the US Government. The U-2 pilot was captured. Pieces of the plane and its surveillance equipment were displayed in the media by the Russians. The saber rattling by the two nuclear powers made the world and me nervous. I wondered whether I would become an adult and have a family, or if the world as we knew it would end.

The world did not end but my sophomore year did. It turned out to be a true year of foolishness. I am not proud of my decisions, and fortunately no one got hurt. There are other stories that could be told, but the point is, I certainly was sophomoric that school year.

The House Painter

A house painter lived just across the alley from our house. His name was Orville Miksch. I regularly saw him load his early

1950's Pontiac sedan with paint and brushes going into the trunk and ladders tied on the top. Off he went to paint. In the evening he returned to clean up his brushes and paint buckets. He folded up his drop cloths. Sometimes he added thinner to the buckets and lit a fire to burn the layers of paint off the sides of his paint buckets. This intrigued me. At times, I went over to his yard and watched the process more closely. Finally, I got up enough nerve to ask if he needed a helper. It was spring, and he had a lot of work to accomplish that summer while the weather was nice. Mr. Miksch said he could use my help. We agreed that I could start when school ended.

I knew that I needed to tell my existing employers about my new summer job. One evening when I arrived at the theater to run the projectors, I informed Mr. Jones that I needed to quit being his farm hand. I told him I was going to be a painter for Mr. Miksch. Mr. Jones quickly understood and agreed that I did not need to work on his farm. He also graciously agreed to still let me run the projectors when I wanted. I later informed my supervisor at J.C. Penney's that I could no longer work several evenings a week after school let out for summer.

When summer came, I bought a couple pairs of painter overalls at Penney's. Painter overalls have a big pocket on the chest to hold a paint rag at the ready. The overalls were off-white canvas. In addition, painters need a screwdriver to open paint buckets, a hammer to drive nails in flush to the walls before they are painted, and a scraper to scrape curled and chipped paint. These items were carried in the overalls at all times.

The first thing Orville taught me was how to load his car. Everything had its place even though to the inexperienced eye, it looked like a chaotic mess. For a new job, we started at one of the stores downtown that sold paint. I learned that Mr. Miksch bought his paint for his jobs at every store in town that sold paint. I guessed it was good small town politics to patronize all the local merchants. While the paint was mixed in the paint shakers, Orville and the merchant talked about small town politics and gossip.

The next thing I was taught was how to set up the ladders

properly. We used sets of small step ladders, tall step ladders, medium extension ladders, and long extension ladders. We put a long plank between those sets of ladders. One of the planks had a wire stiffener underneath because it was twelve feet long. The planks rested on the rungs of the step ladders. When using the extension ladders, a ladder jack was used to hold the plank. Oftentimes both Orville and I worked on the same set of ladders and plank. He taught me about having "ladder legs" which is something like sea legs on a boat.

    He taught me how to hold my brush so my fingers would not get tired. He taught me how to cut straight lines on the edge of glass windows. I learned how to glaze windows in preparation for painting. I learned how to fix broken screens and paint the wire screen with thinned paint. I learned how to avoid drips and runs in the paint. I learned all about being a house painter.

    We painted houses all over town. Sometimes we stained wood shingles on roofs of houses. We stood on the sloping roofs using a roof jack. Roof jacks were built so the pointed feet stuck on the roof and the board that was fixed to the metal frame was level on the sloping roof. We stood on the roof jack or placed our paint bucket on the board of the roof jack. Also, we used the long extension ladder that had the metal bracket that the other extension slid into when the two extensions were used together. The extension ladder bracket was hooked over the galvanized ridge row of the roof. Then, we stood on the angled ladder, which laid flat on the roof. If the pitch of the roof was moderate, we just stood on the sloped shingles—carefully.

    One day we were painting a one-story house. The roof shingles needed to be stained green. We were using the ladder with its bracket fixed over the top galvanized ridge row. As I worked from the top of the roof down the roof slope, I moved down the ladder for footing. What I had not noticed was the roof had a slight crown in its surface. When I had worked my way near the bottom of the ladder, my weight on the ladder lifted the top part of the ladder away from the ridge row. The ladder bracket slipped off the ridge row; down the roof went the ladder, my bucket of stain in my hand, and me with my paint brush in the other hand.

Below me was a broken down fence with steel fence posts sticking out of the ground. I knew the fence was down there, but I was not sure where the posts were. Off the roof the paint equipment and I flew. I pushed myself away from the ladder, and looked for the fence post as I fell. Fortunately, I missed the fence posts and landed out from the house on the ground. Instantly, the bucket of stain hit me on the head. The stain covered me. I thought the damage was done, but then the ladder, which shot out beyond me, fell over and hit me on the head again. I sat there covered with the ladder and green stain. I looked back up at Mr. Miksch on the roof. He had a surprised and concerned look, but he began laughing as soon as he realized my pride was the only thing hurting. I took off my fairly new overalls that were now green down the front (I wore other clothes underneath), and Mr. Miksch took me home for the day. It took a lot of paint thinner and several days of scrubbing before I stopped looking like the Jolly Green Giant.

In late July, Orville and I painted a barn. Of course we were painting it "barn red." It was huge. We did all our painting by brush. We always planned our painting so we could work on the shady side of each building. Sometimes best laid plans do not always work out. On one of the mornings we were working in the full July sun. We stopped for lunch. Our car had been sitting in the hot sun. I ate my sandwich which had lots of mayonnaise in it. I drank lots of water. After our normal lunch break, we went back to work. By mid-afternoon I was as sick as I could be. Orville drove me home, suspecting my lunch spoiled from the heat in the car.

When we arrived home, there were cars all around our home.

Barb, Jim, Hazel, Jesse, and Ken

I was told Grandpa Hesman died; the day was July 26, 1960. Grandpa Hesman had been in the new hospital because he had become so weak that he was incapacitated in a lot of ways. He was seventy-nine-years-old. The funeral was held, and then he was buried at the Red Cloud Cemetery next to Grandma Hesman. Finally, the reddish Hesman gravestone that Grandpa had spent so many hours staring at contained both Grandma and Grandpa Hesman's names on its shiny surface. They were together again.

As the summer continued, the evenings were filled with cruising, swimming, fixing cars, and girls. As it turned out, I did attract a high school sweetheart. We had many good times together. I just could not see us cruising in that rusty '49 Ford.

At the end of summer, I noticed a nice looking '54 Chevy sitting on the used car lot. I had saved enough to buy it for the $400 price tag. My "new" Chevy was all green, had lots of chrome, and a good radio. Unfortunately, the engine was a straight six, which made the car a little under-powered. But, it was nicer than the Ford, and it was mine. I put on new seat covers and disc hub caps in order to start the school year in style.

Upper Class Style

Eleventh grade was more interesting. I went out for football. No more smoking and late nights out. Coach Mills and Coach Peck were our leaders. The practices were time consuming and took a lot of energy. I was not a fast runner and not very tall. But from lifting bales of hay, I was quite strong. I was suited to take the position of relief center; my number was 67. When classes were finished in the afternoons, the football team members were required to walk to the football field. It was a twelve block walk with football shoes, all the pads, helmet, and uniform. We were always quite a sight as we made our way across town. When we got to the field, we did exercises and some scrimmaging. Then we walked back to the high school to the locker room and showered. On game nights we rode the bus to the field or to the other town in which we were to compete. The season's results were not so good: six losses, two wins, and a tie. I did not take the results personally, but I was part of the team that should have done better. We had some good times, some disciplined times, and some painful times.

I joined the RC Club, the athletic club of the school. I took all the required courses for junior year. My girlfriend and I studied together a lot. My grades were better, thanks to her. Each year the junior class put on a number of short plays. I participated in *The Haunted Bookshop*. I really hated being in plays. I feared that I would forget my lines, but I got through it.

Because I learned I could not hit a basket and did not enjoy humiliation, I did not go out for basketball. However, I did go out for track and field in the spring. My upper body strength made shot put and discus an obvious fit for my field events. The problem with track and field that I failed to think through is that everyone is required to run and run and run.

The Last Hurrahs of the Last Summer

Not surprising, the summer between my junior and senior year was filled with work in an effort to earn spending money. Work was fun at times, though, because Orville hired a friend of mine to help us paint. Now he had two teenagers to coach and mentor as we completed various paint jobs around town. Besides working, other activities were spontaneous with friends. We went roller skating at Inavale. We went to the stock car races at the Franklin Fair Grounds. Sometimes we got some thrills by driving over the steep and sharp drops on the roads northwest of town; I think they were called the Seven Devil Hills. We swung through Guide Rock then traveled back on the river road. Occasionally, we drove our cars to the Indian Princes' gravesite on the south side of town. From there we could see the whole Republican Valley and Red Cloud area. Many times we would go to the old Burlington Depot and into the Beanery cafe which was a high school hang out for many of us. If there were carnivals in any of the nearby towns, we checked them out. In Hastings we went to a drive-in movie theater some weekends. Of course, we spent time at the Sugar and Spice or at Lockhart's Malt Shop. Most of us saw all the movies at the State Theater.

One night at the Hastings Drive-in Theater, two of us couples were watching the movie. At some point during the show there was the usual intermission so people could get refreshments and use the restroom. I was in the restroom using a urinal. A muscular looking guy came to use the urinal next to me. He asked me if I was afraid of him. I looked at him and decided to say no. Suddenly, he was all over me. It did not take too long for me to decide I was in harm's way. Using my football tackling skills, I went up under his waist, lifted him off his feet and slammed him into the restroom wall. He was stunned for a moment, so I walked outside into the crowd. I went back to the car licking my wounds and was glad I got out of there as soon as I did.

A month or so later, Orville, my friend, and I were painting a new house east of Red Cloud. One day a concrete construction crew from Hastings showed up. One member of that crew was the same guy that I met in the drive-in restroom. We recognized each other, but managed to avoid each other while they finished their concrete work. I told Orville about the incident in Hastings; he was glad I held my cool while they were at the worksite.

When people work side-by-side on ladders and scaffolds day after day, they share a lot of stories and thoughts. Orville taught us about being on time, delivering good quality work to our customers, caring for our family, standing by our word, being responsible and trustworthy, having high ethical standards, being positive, taking care of our tools, knowing right and wrong, and being a steady person whom others could depend on at all times. Orville certainly exemplified all those qualities and traits for me. I could see that other community leaders and business people respected Orville for the same reasons. He was a great mentor for a young man.

Fire in Red Cloud!

Red Cloud had a siren downtown that could be heard all over town. At noon the siren sounded. Everyone could set his or her watch and go to lunch. The siren was used to send out an alarm for the volunteer firemen.

On Saturday afternoon, August 5th, the siren went off again and again. Fire trucks from our town, and towns around, could be heard making their way downtown. The scene at the junction of 281 and 136 was chaos. Fire trucks were everywhere. Fire hoses were strung out down the streets to every fire hydrant in the area.

The three story brick Potter-Wright building on the southeast corner of the intersection was ablaze. Billowing, heavy black smoke rose high into the sky. Water was shooting through the air onto the roof and into the windows of the building. Fire trucks from Guide Rock and Franklin were called to join the Red Cloud fire department. The firemen were climbing on ladders and struggling to lay out all the hoses and other equipment. I had never seen such a fire and convergence of rescue equipment. Well, maybe on TV, but not in real life.

The fire appeared to be concentrated on the top floor. All at once, part of the roof caved in and flames shot higher. Water ran out of the building doors and into the streets. Finally, toward evening, the fire was contained. The visiting firemen and equipment left for their own towns. The Red Cloud volunteer firemen sprayed water into the night to insure the fire was suppressed.

The next morning everyone downtown surveyed the

damage and stood around in small groups talking about the amazing disaster of the day before. All the while, the Red Cloud Volunteer Firemen were picking up their equipment and putting it back onto the fire trucks.

The building seemed just to sit there for weeks. The source of the fire was never determined. It started on the third floor, which had been a ballroom and formerly was used by the Masons and Eastern Star lodges. I had seen the room during a Rainbow Girls ceremony during the summer. Now, just a blackened shell on the top floor with water damage around the windows and doors of the two lower floors could be seen from the street. Many townspeople speculated on what might happen to the once grand building.

Eventually, construction workers began the demolition of the top floor. Truckloads of burned wood, broken glass, layers of plaster, water soaked furniture, and other materials were taken away. The brick walls were removed down to the top level of the second floor. At the top of the second floor, a new roof and building trim was installed. All the water and smoke damaged walls inside the building were repaired or replaced. The three-story building was now a two-story building.

Orville Miksch was granted the contract to clean and repaint all the repaired rooms in the building. We looked through the whole building to determine the magnitude of the job to clean, paint the walls, and refinish the woodwork. The existing walls and woodwork had water damage and smoke stains. The whole building had a strong musty, burnt smell that just about knocked a person over. We bought gallons and gallons of paint. Also, we bought a supply of Tri-Sodium Phosphate for washing down existing woodwork and walls. We bought a good amount of shellac to seal in the water stains. In those days, we did not have effective stain blocker paints like we have today.

After mixing the Tri-Sodium Phosphate with water to create a dilute acid solution, we donned rubber gloves and washed all the surfaces that were not replaced in an effort to reduce the smoke and water damage. Even though we had gloves, the cleaning liquid got under our gloves, ran down our arms, and sometime splashed on our face. The result was a slight acid burn which left stinging red marks on our skin. As we completed cleaning all the surfaces, the burnt smell disappeared from the building. We shellacked all the remaining water stains on the existing walls. Finally, we were ready to prime and paint all the walls and refinish the woodwork throughout the whole building. The paint job for that building was the largest project I had worked on with Orville.

A New Dream Car

That summer my parents took a big step and bought a '59 Desoto Sportsman, two-door hard top. I do not know what got into them, but that car was beautiful. It was pinkish beige and white. That car was a city block long and had fins that seemed to be higher than the roof of the car. It had power brakes and power steering. Chrome was everywhere, inside and out. The seats inside seemed like four people could sit side by side across the seats. The inside mirror was mounted on the dash. It had twin rear view mirrors outside on the front fenders and two rear aerials. The car had front swing out seats that let you sit down before you swung into the normal driving position. The engine was a big 361 V-8 with a push button transmission on the dash.

My '54 Chevy looked pretty homely setting in the driveway beside the Desoto. Of course, I created all kinds of excuses why it would be good for me to take the Desoto out and about. Chrysler products were not the choice of cars for teenagers; but, when I had that car; it was pretty easy to get others to go along for a ride.

chapter fifteen
senior year
the nebraska boy grown up

Finally, our senior year arrived. We were the upper class of the Red Cloud High School. Unfortunately, that meant making decisions about our futures.

There was the question of college or not. If college was in the cards, how would it be financed? Which college should be the college of choice? Were my grades good enough to even get into college? How would I do on the scholastic tests that should be taken? What would I do if I did not go to college?

I came to the conclusion my future required college. No one in my family had ever gone to college. I knew my vision for my future would not be one my parents thought was possible. I knew I would need to pay for it on my own or get scholarships.

I decided that I needed to work as many part-time jobs as I could handle to save for college. Sports would not be in the cards my senior year. My grades had to be better than the past and good enough to be accepted in a college. I thought industrial arts should be my major, and I would plan to become a teacher.

I turned eighteen in August, which meant I needed to go to the local draft board and register. That task was a sobering one. Would I join the armed forces? Would that postpone college or was that a way for me to go to college? At the time there was no war going on. I got my draft card in the mail and put it in my wallet. The card just stayed there, but it was a reminder of a potential obligation or a possible opportunity.

Every time I thought of what it would be like to join the service, I wondered if I would ever make it through the shot line. I heard stories about young men lined up bare-naked with people looking at the front and back of you. Nurses worked on both sides sticking needles in each arm for one shot after another. If any person fainted, they just laid there until they came around. I thought it may take days for me to get all the shots if I fainted each time. Boot camp sounded just as bad.

Senior Year Changes

This school year was shaping up differently. My girlfriend and I split up. Our future together was not to be. Because of that change, the social aspects of high school shifted for me. I participated in the Lettermen's Club and was the Treasurer.

The senior class play was always a big event to plan and in which to participate. The senior play was called *Off the Track*. I played the part of the train station master. I participated in the Kearney Scholastics program. Out of that I received a Baldwin Scholarship for Kearney State Teacher's College. Each year a school annual was created and published by the senior class. I was the Business Manager for the annual staff.

The Class of '62 Motto was a good reality statement for me. "We know what we are, but know not what we may be." But in my case at least I had a vision of what I thought I should be.

Partway through the school year, my parents declared they decided to go back to Oregon. They were out in Oregon as a young couple and wanted to return. My upcoming graduation felt like the appropriate transition time for their return to Oregon. They wanted to know what my plans were for after high school.

That was the big question. Since my parents said they were

leaving Nebraska, it became quite clear that going to college in Nebraska would be difficult, if not impossible. I would have no immediate family in Nebraska other than grandparents who were quite old and aunts, uncles, and cousins. I would have no home, and my job was not where the college in Nebraska was located. After I thought about their question, I said I would go to Oregon with them.

For the rest of the school year, I kept a pretty low profile. I studied and worked. I went to the school games. On weekend nights, I joined in on some activities with my friends.

Soon it was time for our class to prepare for graduation. We made graduation event decisions like having the graduation ceremony in the city park, which might have been a first and maybe a last. We knew our colors were Royal Blue and White. Nothing strange about the colors except we had the choice of caps and gowns made of cloth or "paper." Being the cutting edge thinkers that we were, we chose "paper." There were many reasons for our choice, like we could keep our caps and gowns; they would make good napkins at an after graduation party; they were absorbent, so we could wipe our proud parent's tears of joy from their face; the cost was cheaper; and probably no other class had or would use paper for their graduation gowns. I personally thought the idea of using disposable caps and gowns was a novel idea and reflected the uniqueness of our class.

One of my buddies knew I was into making money, so he invited me to join him on a road construction crew the week that the seniors were out of school between the Baccalaureate service and the Commencement.

Working on a Road Crew

His offer sounded interesting to me. I had never worked on a road construction crew. Sure enough, when we got to the construction site, they were hiring extra help. I was hired for the week to run an asphalt rolling machine.

The machine had two large steel drums for wheels. The drum was full of water for weight. In a couple minutes I was trained to run the machine back and forth on the hot asphalt. The steering bar was the mechanism for the operator to move the machine left and right. There was a forward and reverse lever, a brake, a throttle lever, and a seat to sit on. The machine was easy to run and kind of fun at first. At mid-week it was quite boring.

The sun that week was blazing hot. The hot asphalt made more heat, and the freshly laid road reflected more intense heat.

At the end of the week we completed a road that finally intersected with an existing highway. In those days, the asphalt laying machine went straight forward. There were no turns made except long gentle ones. The intersection needed to be fanned out by hand with rakes and shovels. When the asphalt was spread out on the ground, the rollers compacted it filling in the edges of the intersection. The workers had to get into the dump truck and shovel the hot asphalt out of the truck by hand. I was drafted to be in the truck. However, my shirt was on the roller machine. I could not delay getting in the truck. I worked in the hot truck under the blazing sun for a couple hours. When we were done with the intersection, the job was done.

Graduation Day

We drove home knowing that the Commencement was that weekend. By evening, my shoulders and back were flaming red and burning like fire rising off my skin. By Sunday I was a mess. My shoulders were raw. What could I do but put bandages on my shoulders and put on my shirt? At the park we graduates met on the tennis courts. People were hugging and congratulating each other. Some slaps on the shoulder practically took me to the ground. That was a painful process for me, but I kept a forced smile on my face. The ceremony was too long for my condition, but I got through it. I did not celebrate that night.

Go West Young Man!

The summer after graduation was busy. My parents made their plans to move to Oregon. They decided to move to Coos Bay, Oregon on the southwestern coastal region. My brother and his family were living there. It seemed like an obvious place to start over as Oregonians. My parents made arrangements with my sister and brother-in-law to swing through Minot, North Dakota so they could travel to Oregon with my parents. All of us planned to relocate to Coos Bay. Their trip was to take place in October when my brother-in-law's tour of duty at Minot ended.

I told Orville about my plans to start fresh in Oregon with my parents. I told him I would be leaving in August. My friend, who also worked for Orville, agreed to drive out to Oregon with me. Orville was supportive and happy that I and my friend planned to work through the summer with him. We talked a lot about going to a new part of the country. Orville could not imagine being anywhere but right there in Red Cloud.

The thought of leaving was like planning to dive into a black hole. What about a job? What about college? What would Oregon be like? Who were the people that I would meet? Would my '54 Chevy make it? None of these questions had answers.

Knowing that we were all leaving the area brought finality to our life as Nebraskans. We had family reunions to say our goodbyes to all the aunts, uncles, cousins, and grandparents. I wondered if I would see my grandparents again. We said our farewells to our friends at Zion Lutheran Church. As I went around town, I let my friends know I was leaving. They shared their plans as well. I canceled my application to attend the Kearney State Teacher's College and canceled my request for the scholarship that I had received. Of course, I went to Marvin Jones and Ernie Warner to share my plans with them.

At the Texaco, I spent time preparing the Chevy for the long trip. I tuned the engine, lubed the car, put on new shocks, fan belt, brakes, and tires. The trustworthy Chevy seemed ready to go. One afternoon late in the summer, I pulled out of the Texaco Station to head home. As the engine revved up to change gears, a loud bang sounded out in the front end of the car. As I looked down the hood of the car, a hole could be seen right in the front, top side of the hood. The engine was idling rough. I pulled off to the curb and opened the hood. A fan blade had flown off its hub and through the hood of my car! It was a four-inch jagged gash. The exploded metal stood up about an inch from the surface of the hood. That scar really made the whole car look bad. It was like having a wart on your nose. You could not help but stare at that wart. I was sad. Was this a sign of things to come as I made plans to travel to Oregon?

No money was available to fix the hole in the hood of my car and repaint it. So I tried to ignore it. On the day after August 24th, my 19th birthday, my friend and I took off from Red Cloud. We had our clothes and some food to eat on the way. We had maps of places we'd never seen before. We laid our course to make the three-day journey.

Westward Ho!

We decided to take the mountainous route west. I had my tools and oil in the trunk, in case something happened to the car. My mom had bought us a brand new one gallon thermos jug so we always had water for us or the car. We had said our goodbyes to our families and boldly went where we had not gone before.

We traveled north to Grand Island. Then we turned west and headed for Estes Park, Colorado. Our objective was to cross the Rocky Mountains at one of the highest passes. On the map The Rocky Mountain National Park seemed like an exciting route to pick for two Nebraska boys. As we climbed the foothills of the Rockies, we thought the mountainous path would be no sweat. When we started climbing the mountain range into Estes Park however, we knew we did not know what we truly did not know.

The Chevy was huffing and puffing to make the climb higher and higher. We went slower and slower, oftentimes creeping along in second gear. When we hit the high mountains, the road turned to gravel in spots and there were patches of snow in

August along the side of the road. The road wound around mountain tops and down into mountain top valleys, all the while taking us higher and higher. We were in and out of low-hanging clouds that gave the landscape a gray, damp unwelcoming look. Finally, we came to the Fall River Pass which is 11,796 feet above sea level (more than a half mile higher than the South Pass that the Oregon Trail emigrants took). We drove along Trail Ridge road and soon came to Milner Pass which was 10,758 feet above sea level. At that altitude, the old '54 Chevy was gasping for air but had certainly passed its first big test of endurance. We saw incredible mountains that we had never dreamed about. Over the Continental Divide we went. For the first time, we saw the water in creeks and rivers flowing west instead of east.

I was glad I put on new brakes! Going down the west side of the Divide required constant braking and shifting into lower gears. We dropped down into Hot Sulphur Springs and filled up with gas. We thought we had seen the worst of the challenging mountain roads.

We started off and soon found ourselves climbing back up into a mountain range that took us right back up to the Continental Divide—again! We went over Muddy Pass (8,772 feet above sea level) and Rabbit Ears Pass (9,426 feet above sea level). I developed a lot of respect for that old '54 Chevy. It just kept on going. We descended the west side of the Rockies down into Steamboat Springs, Colorado.

The drive was long and relatively flat as we traveled across northwestern Colorado into northeastern Utah. We traveled across the Uintah-Ouray Indian Reservation. From there we drove through the Uinta Mountains into the east side of Salt Lake City. We slept in the car and only stopped for gas and supplies.

At Salt Lake City, Utah we took a break. We visited the Mormons' Salt Lake Temple. Never had we seen such magnificent architecture. We visited the Utah Capitol building. Then, it was time to move on toward Idaho and Oregon. We traveled through Twin Falls and on to Boise. We spent hours and hours driving in the open countryside with sagebrush as far as our eyes could see.

At the Ontario, Oregon border, we followed Highway 20 across eastern Oregon into Burns and Bend. On the map we noticed a round lake in the middle of the Crater Lake National Park. We thought it looked interesting. We turned south out of Bend on Highway 97.

The Crater Lake Adventure

In a couple hours, we drove into the park and started our climb up the mountainous Cascade Range terrain. With great surprise we crested over the brim and spied the most magnificent view of a giant crater imaginable. The walls of the crater dove straight down to the bright sky blue water. The water was a blue that only God could have created. No human artist could have created such a beautiful brilliant hue. There was a small Island near the western edge of the crater. Trees grew out of the volcanic soil all around. At a parking lot nearest to the island, on the edge of the giant cauldron, we looked in amazement at the crater's perfect circle. Coming from Nebraska, we could not have imagined such an awesome sight existed in our country.

It was a warm, sunny mid-day in late August. And after looking at the map, it seemed we had enough time to spend a few hours at Crater Lake and still make it to Coos Bay by evening. I said to my traveling partner, "Let's take my thermos jug and get some Crater Lake water." It looked so clear and inviting. We got the thermos and locked the car. Over the side of the crater we went. We did not know we should not go over the side. The slope was so steep that we slid on rock and shale for nearly forty-five minutes. It was like skiing, but on sliding shale rock. Finally, we got near the shore of the water. I was slightly ahead of my adventurous partner.

Suddenly, I heard a loud rattling. I froze and told my partner to do the same. I carefully looked around, thinking the sound came from a rattlesnake lying in the dusty shale rock in which we were standing. The sound got louder then decreased. Then it again got louder and then decreased. The time seemed so long; suddenly a large bug, like a locust, flew up and away. I was relieved, but felt stupid. When I looked back at my friend, I looked up and out of the crater for the first time. I could not see the rim or the tops of the trees that hung on the side of the crater. I began to wonder what we had done to ourselves.

We went ahead to the water's edge. The lake bottom fell deeply into the clear blue water. The water quietly lapped against the shore line. We could see it was a short distance to the small island. It gave us no comfort, though, because we knew we were all alone in a place that we should not be. We filled the thermos jug with cold, clear Crater Lake water.

Our sense of urgency grew as we surveyed the shale rock slide on which we descended. It looked like the most logical way back up the steep slope to the top. As we started climbing up the shale, we realized it was an impossible pathway. As much as we climbed up; we slid back down. We made no progress.

We decided to try an ascent, to the side of the shale rock slide, straight up into the trees. The soil easily sloughed off the slope. It was dry and dusty. We struggled for firm footing and a solid handhold. We climbed from tree to tree holding onto their trunks. The trees were the only way of staying on the side of the crater. We made our way to steep rock ledges crusted with the soft soil. From time to time we took drinks from the water jug. We traveled along the ledges until we reached another tree or rock to make more upward progress. At times we were not sure if we could actually reach the top. We still could not see the tops of the trees or the rim of the crater.

The shore line kept dropping farther away from our position on the crater wall. We climbed unsafely along the ledges and slopes for a couple hours. We continued to drink water from the jug. We did not talk much because we knew this was serious business. Finally, we saw we were up as high as the tops of the trees and we were getting closer to the rim. At that point we ran out of trees on which to hold.

We simply scratched our way in the soft soil and rock to the top of the rim.

When we crested the rim, we climbed over the parking lot log fence and sat on the logs for a moment. We were sweaty, covered with the fine dust, and exhausted. My new thermos jug was empty because it was our only source of water on the long trip back to the top. The jug was dented and punctured on its outside from all the banging on the rocks and ledges. We threw the jug in the trash barrel. People in the parking lot looked at us in a surprised and curious way.

When we got our breath and composure back, we went to the car. We wiped as much dust and mud off our faces as possible. We drove away from the beautiful and dangerous crater toward Coos Bay, Oregon.

At that time, we did not know descending the crater was against park rules. There were only a few paths to the water which park rangers used at the bottom of the crater. Tourists only go on those paths with ranger supervision. I have been to Crater Lake since our adventurous trip and wonder, first of all, why? Why did we think we could do something so idiotic? Secondly, I wonder how we survived the climb. God had more plans for us is the only answer I can surmise.

About ten o'clock that evening, we arrived in Coos Bay, Oregon; the old '54 Chevy made it with no break down or flat tire. We found my brother's house and knocked on the front door. His wife, Helen, came to the door and saw two beaten down, dirty, and hungry teenagers looking for a place to stay. That night, I wrote my mother a post card telling of our adventure. Here is what it said:

Dear Mom & Dad,

We made it Wed. about 8:00pm. We stopped in Salt Lake and went through the Capitol and the Mormon Temple. Then we left and the next stop besides sleep was Crater Lake. We climbed down into the lake crater. Boy that was the hardest and longest climb I ever attempted. We did get some water out of the lake though. That was the most beautiful sight I've ever seen before. It is unexplainable. But the water is just as blue or even bluer and prettier than this picture is. It looked like something that God took special pains to make. We made the trip without any trouble not even a flat. Helen says hello. Ken isn't home yet so I haven't seen him yet. Well, I'll write a little later. –Jim

PS. It looks just like a big bowl of blue water. If you don't pull trailer, try to see Crater Lake.

The Ocean

The next morning we recovered enough to continue our adventure. We traveled clear across the western United States, but had not yet seen the Pacific Ocean. We decided we wanted to fish in the great western pond. We bought some fishing equipment and were told we did not need a license to fish in the ocean.

We headed off to a place called Shore Acres, a beautiful garden park on the cliffs of the Pacific Coast. The day was sunny and breezy. When the first sight of the Pacific Ocean registered in our brains, it blew our minds. The blue Pacific Ocean, with rolling waves hitting the craggy rocks with explosive force, was a sight not to be accurately imagined. The salty spray from the crashing waves was surprisingly refreshing. The water receded off the rocks only to build up and hit the rocks without end.

At Shore Acres Park on the southern coast of Oregon, the shoreline had steep cliffs and coves for the water to continuously carve and explore. The sandstone rock looked like Swiss cheese where the water had eaten smooth, round holes into the surface of the rock. The rock formations allowed us to climb down next to the water. The crashing sound from the ebb and flow of waves on the rocks appropriately made this

Nebraska boy nervous. There were a series of small waves, and then a larger wave snuck up to the rocks splashing it unexpectedly. Those waves were dangerous for us neophytes to the ocean. Again, we didn't realize the power and danger of God's West Coast creation.

We sized up the situation and were ready to go fishing. We carried purchased bait in a jar, which I never found to be too attractive for fishing. But it was all we had for our first fishing trip in the ocean. We found a spot between the rocks where the waves moved in and out. We started casting. We instantly had a hit. We pulled it in. It was an ugly reddish, black spotted fish about ten to twelve inches long. Immediately we caught another one; and another. We decide maybe the ocean had too many of these fish, so perhaps they were trash fish like our carp back in Nebraska. They were fun to catch but we threw most of them back. After a while we decided to go back to my brother's house and be sociable. We took only several of those fish home with us just to see what these abundant fish were.

My brother was happy to see the fish. We filleted the fish; the meat was a pale blue. When we fried the fish the meat turned white like any other white fish. They turned out to be great tasting fish; a valuable and desired catch.

The next day, my friend and I headed back out to Shore Acres thinking it was a cinch to catch more of the abundant mystery fish. We fished for hours and never caught any kind of fish, not even one. What made matters worse was one of those sneaky waves flooded the rock I was on and took all my new tackle with it as it rolled back out to sea. I scampered up the side of the rocks to save myself. Fishing in the ocean did not seem so easy anymore. We had a lot to learn about the ocean.

Fate

On Sunday morning we agreed to go to my brother and sister-in-law's Lutheran church. We arrived at the church in plenty of time. My brother had duties to take care of. My sister-in-law disappeared to get their kids into their Sunday school classes.

My friend and I were milling around in the narthex of the church. At one point, the outside doors opened up. In walked two gorgeous girls. One was a blond with white cat eye glasses. The other was a brunette with a really nice smile. I thought both girls were stunning. I could not take my eyes off the blond. In the back of my mind I knew why I had come to Oregon. I would marry her.

My future in Oregon was looking good!

epilogue
the rest of the story

My friend and I got jobs in a plywood mill. The union struck the mill a couple months later and put us out of work. We walked the picket line. My friend decided to return to Nebraska on a bus.

I went to work in a plumbing and heating shop in Coos Bay, Oregon. But I didn't let my dream of going to college rest. I enrolled in the local community college.

On July 16, 1965 the blond haired girl I first saw in the Christ Lutheran Church in Coos Bay, Oregon, and I married in that same church.

We have two daughters who are grown and married. We have three wonderful grandchildren and are hoping for more.

Yes, for better or worse, my wife, Ann, accepts my eccentricity of not dangling anything over the edge of our bed because the alligators continue to accompany me on my journey.

The Coos Bay/North Bend Southwestern Oregon Community College was the college in which I received an Associate Degree in Business in 1965. I transferred to the University of Oregon at Eugene the same year. After four years of working full-time, caring for my young family, and going to school, I graduated with a Bachelor of Science in Business Administration in March of 1969.

In May of 1969, I was hired by Crown Simpson Pulp Company as the Assistant Personnel Manager in Eureka,

California. In 1975, I was promoted and transferred to a large Crown Zellerbach (CZ) paper mill in Camas, Washington. One of the products made in that mill was the kind of paper that was used in our graduation gowns. I was the Safety and Worker's Compensation Manager.

In 1979, I was promoted and transferred to the CZ paper mill in Port Angeles, Washington. There, on the Juan De Fuca Straights, I experienced the best salmon, shrimping, and cod fishing anywhere.

In 1982, I transferred to the West Linn, Oregon CZ paper mill as the Human Resources Manager. West Linn is across the river from Oregon City, which was the official Oregon Trail destination.

In 1985, I joined the CZ Chemical Products Division as the Human Resources Manager. After a hostile takeover of Crown Zellerbach by a British financier, Sir James Goldsmith, the major manufacturing assets were purchased by James River Corporation. James River Corporation transferred me to their Nonwovens Division in Simpsonville, South Carolina as Human Resources Manager.

In 1990, James River sold the Nonwovens Business to a holding company in Switzerland. I was promoted to Director, Human Resources for Fiberweb North America, a subsidiary of the international business. In 1995, a British holding company took control of the Swiss holding company. A re-organization eliminated my position in January 1996.

In May 1996, I was hired and relocated to a large International Paper (IP) mill in Jay, Maine as Manager, Human Resources. We lived in the historical village of Wilton, Maine. After nine years, International Paper relocated us back to Simpsonville, South Carolina where I worked as a Human Resources consultant to the many IP mills across the US.

On January 1, 2008 I retired from International Paper and now enjoy retirement in Simpsonville, South Carolina with my blond-haired girl at my side. We are members of the Messiah Lutheran Church, Mauldin, South Carolina.

In 2009, I joined the "Family Authors Club," with this, my first published book. My sister, Barbara Knight, has authored seven children's books. The series is titled "Penny the Mustang Pony." My daughter, Melissa Leembruggen, is also a published author of several children's books.

endnotes

Note #1: Webster County Records show that Grandpa Hesman's father, Vensal Heseman who later changed his name to Venzel Hesman, obtained his citizenship and land in Webster County. On October 22, 1876, Vensal Heseman filed for record in Bloomington, Nebraska an application for a homestead under the May 20, 1862 Homestead Act to secure homesteads to actual settlers on the public domain. Vensal Heseman became a Naturalized Citizen of the United States in Red Cloud, Nebraska in the Webster County Court House on November 20, 1883. On November 23, 1883 Vensal Heseman made his final $2 payment for his homestead entry of 80 acres of land. On January 15, 1885 he was awarded the Patent Record for a Homestead Certificate No. 4503, under the application 4024. His parcel of land was on the northwest corner of Section Twelve of Potsdam Precinct two miles east of Blue Hill, Nebraska. It was on this homestead property in a dugout that Grandpa Hesman was born and raised.

On May 7, 1888, Venzel Hesman paid $220 for an additional forty acres of land on the southwest corner of Section 1. On June 23, 1908 Venzel Hesman wrote his last will and testament wherein the homestead would be sold after his death to pay all outstanding debt and the remainder divided amongst his children and grandchildren. This was the beginning of the Hesman Webster County farming families.

On a visit to Nebraska, my wife and I visited the Homestead Monument in Beatrice, Nebraska. We were instructed on how to seek out Homestead Records from National Archives in Washington D.C. www.archives.gov. This service is available to anyone who would like to learn more about the conditions in which their ancestors survived or failed to survive. These documents hold valuable clues for us who are interested in the beginnings of our early frontiers.

Records for Venzel Hesman revealed all the details for successfully securing his Land Patent #4503, even the details of the size of the dugout. It was 11 feet by 15 feet and then increased to 12 feet by 16 feet. That is where my Grandpa Hesman lived as a young boy. The Homestead Records show that in addition to the family dugout, other improvements were a stable, granary, corncrib, hog pen, a wall, approximately 1000 forest trees, and thirty fruit trees for a total value of $200. In addition to Venzel Hesman, a wife and five children lived on that land starting in June 1877.

Note #2: Additional Family Homestead Searches revealed that my mother's paternal Father, Vernon H. Thayer, acquired a Land Patent #258606 in Loup County, Nebraska in April, 1912 under the Homestead Act of 1862. My mother's grandfather Floyd A. Thayer received his Land Patent #1426653 in Loup County in July, 1910. To date, no Homestead Land Patents have been discovered for the Hager or Crawford side of our five generations of family.

Notes #3: From time to time my wife and I have returned to Red Cloud. The high school reunions have been the primary reasons for our return to my hometown. Seeing my classmates, class of 1962, and other friends has been rewarding and caused many memories to come to the forefront of my mind. We always drive up and down all the streets remembering all the houses Orville and I painted, and the houses where my family and I lived. My wife has been patient as I have told her many of the details mentioned in this book. We walk the main street to see if I can remember the stores that existed in my days, noticing that no businesses have remained the same. A drive through the Red Cloud Cemetery to visit Grandpa and Grandma Hesman's tombstone brings back memories of my heritage. We drive north to see the location of the farm where I was born and to the farm eight miles north where the windmill still stands as a reminder that a farm once existed there.

On each visit to Red Cloud, we visit the Willa Cather bookstore in the renovated Opera House. The staff members always offer the tour to the Opera House stage area. We have seen the many names on the back stage wall of persons who performed, including Willa Cather's name. The renewed Opera House will provide additional generations of memories of the good ole hometown days. Now that I have read some of Willa Cather's books and see the work of the Willa Cather Foundation, I realize what an impact Willa Cather had on Red Cloud and Webster County.

A 2008 trip to Cowles revealed that the white garage building on which we watched movies still stands.

acknowledgements

My wife, Ann, has been helpful to me in many ways. She listened to my hometown stories for over forty-four years of marrage. In addition, she provided ancestry and homestead research for my autobiography records. She encouraged me to keep going on this writing project.

Grant Harner, who lives in Lincoln, Nebraska, helped confirm a number of the memories and situations that I wrote about. Over the years we have met in Lincoln or Red Cloud and spent a lot of time reminiscing about the old days.

On a visit to Red Cloud this last winter, Junior and Carol Glenn hosted us around town and outlying areas. Lots of memories were shared the whole day long.

My mother and sister, who live in Oregon, confirmed some of the stories and provided a number of the pictures used in the book. Of course my mother and sister were major real life characters in the first nineteen years of my life, which is the span of time for this autobiography.

Aunt Irene and Uncle Fred Hesman, who live in Blue Hill, Nebraska, gave me some valuable materials and provided much of the Hesman family history.

Cousins Judy Kirstine, Victor Hesman, and Karen Bailey provided confirmation of some of the situations remembered in this autobiography.

Director Joyce Terhune, of the Webster County Historical Museum provided a number of Genealogy sources for family history and homestead information held both at the Museum and County Courthouse. In addition, Joyce read a draft of my manuscript and offered suggestions for historical accuracy.

Helen Mathew, Past Director of Webster County Historical Museum, read a draft of my manuscript and provided suggestions for historical accuracy.

Barb Kudrna, from the Willa Cather Foundation read my manuscript for accuracy related to the Willa Cather information.

Bruce Fox, 1962 Red Cloud High School Class President, provided editorial comments and provided accurate information about some of the events in Red Cloud during our school years.

Our dear friend Lori Smalley volunteered to take the first editorial cut at the manuscript, which took many hours to straighten me out on grammar and punctuation.

Clay Bridges Publishing provided much guidance and direction on the final draft, design, and production of my book.

Thank you to all who helped with this document.

works cited

"50's Jitterbug History." CU People: Welcome. Web. 5 Jan. 2009. <http://people.cornell.edu/pages/kpl5/fifties_one.html>.

Ambrosek, Elva. "Andreas' History of The State of Nebraska - Webster County Part 1." Web. 8 Dec. 2008. <http://www.kancoll.org/books/andreas_ne/web-ster/webster-p1.html>.

Ambrosek, Elva. "Andreas' History of The State of Nebraska - Webster County Part 3." Web. 8 Dec. 2008. <http://www.kancoll.org/books/andreas_ne/webster/webster-p3.html>.

Ambrosek, Elva. "Andreas' History of The State of Nebraska - Webster County Part 2." Web. 8 Dec. 2008. <http://kancoll.org/books/andreas_ne/webster/webster-p2/html>.

Banks, William N. "History in towns: Deadwood, South Dakota | Magazine Antiques | Find Articles at BNET." Find Articles at BNET | News Articles, Magazine Back Issues & Reference Articles on All Topics. Home & Garden Publications, July 2004. Web. 25 June 2009. <http://findarticles.com/p/articles/mi_m1026/is_1_166/ai_n6142081>.

Banks, William N. "History in towns: Deadwood, South Dakota | Magazine Antiques | Find Articles at BNET." Find Articles at BNET | News Articles, Magazine Back Issues & Reference Articles on All Topics. Home & Garden Publications, July 2004. Web. 25 June 2009. <http://findarticles.com/p/articles/mi_m1026/is_1_166/ai_n6142081/pg_2/?tag=content;coll>.

Beier, Vanessa. "History of Deadwood, South Dakota." Essortment Articles: Free Online Articles on Health, Science, Education & More.. Web. 25 June 2009. <http://www.essortment.com/all/historydeadwood_ricn.htm>.

"Chief Red Cloud - Attractions in Red Cloud, Nebraska - Travel, Lodging, Events, Atractions, Recreation." Travel, Lodging, Attractions, Events, Recreation. Web. 1 Feb. 2009. <http://www.lasr.net/travel/city.php?RedCloud&Nebraska&City_ID=NE0422025&VA=Y&...>.

"Deadwood - A National Historic Landmark." HistoryLink Home - The Deadwood Historic Preservation Commission. Web. 25 June 2009. <http://deadwoodhistorylink.com>.

"A Decade of Fun, Excitement, and Individuality!" The 1950s. Web. 5 Jan. 2009. <http://www.kidsnewsroom.org/elmer/infoCentral/frameset/decade/1950.htm>.

"Dick Clark." History of Rock. Web. 5 Jan. 2009. <http://www.history-of-rock.com/clark.htm>.

"Disasters The Blizzard of 1949 in Nebraska." The Wessels Living History Farm, the Story of Agricultural Innovation. Web. 2 Jan. 2009. <http://www.livinghistoryfarm.org/farmingthe40s/life_30.html>.

"Ed Sullivan Show." The Museum of Broadcast Communications. Web. 5 Jan. 2009. <http://www.museum.tv/archives/etv/E/htmlE/edsullivans/edsullivans.htm>.

"Fire Guts One Of City's Largest Buildings." Red Cloud Chief 17 Aug. 1961, Number 49 ed. Print.

Fort Laramie Facts. The National Park Service. Web. 25 Feb. 2009. <http://www.nps.gov/archive/fola/facts.htm>.

Gibson, Karen B. The Pawnee Farmers and Hunters of the Central Plains (American Indian Nations). New York: Capstone, 2004. Print.

"Harlan County Lake." Web. 21 Jan. 2009. <http://www.nwk.usace.army.mil/hc/LowLake-OldRepublicanCity.cfm>.

"History - Republican City, Nebraska." Welcome to Republican City, Nebraska. Web. 21 Jan. 2009. <http://www.ci.republican-city.ne.us/history.htm>.

Hutt, Sherry. National NAGPRA Program, 30 Jan. 2008. Web. 8 Dec. 2008. <http://edocket.access.gpo.gov/2008/E8-4323.htm>.

Kelly, Martin. "Jefferson and the Louisiana Purchase." About.com. Martin Kelly. Web. 24 June 2009. <http://americanhistory.about.com/od/thomasjefferson/a/tj_lapurchase.htm>.

"Korolev-- Sputnik." NASA History Home Page. Web. 9 Jan. 2009. <http://history.nasa.gov/sputnik/harford.html>.

"Lake - Republican City, Nebraska." Welcome to Republican City, Nebraska. Web. 21 Jan. 2009. <http://www.ci.republican-city.ne.us/lake.htm>.

"Mount Moriah Cemetery - Lawrence County, South Dakota." Cemetery Records Online. Web. 25 June 2009. <http://interment.net/data/us/sd/lawrence/moriah/index.htm>.

"National Historic Trails- Oregon." GORP. Web. 29 Jan. 2009. <http://gorp.away.com/gorp/resource/us_trail/ore.htm>.

"National Park Service - U.S. Department of the Interior. Nebraska: U.S. Department of the Interior, 2007. Print.

"1960 U-2 incident." 1960 U-2 incident - Wikipedia, the free encyclopedia. Wikipedia. Web. 19 Jan. 2009. <http://en.wikipedia.org/wiki/U-2_Crisis_of_1960>.

"1960 U-2 incident." 1960 U-2 incident - Wikipedia, the free encyclopedia. Wikipedia. Web. 25 June 2009. <http://en.wikipedia.org/wiki/1960_U-2_incident>.

"Oregon Trail." Map. Oregon Trail - Map - MSN Encarta. Microsoft Corporation. Web. 29 Jan. 2009. <http://encarta.msn.com/media_461517720/oregon_trail.html>.

"Oregon Trail." Wikipedia, the free encyclopedia. Web. 24 June 2009. <http://en.wikipedia.org/wiki/Oregon_Trail>.

"Pike-Pawnee Village And Historical Marker." Red Cloud, Nebraska Attractions. Web. 1 Feb. 2009.<http://www.lasr.net/travel/city.php?RedCloud&Nebraska&City_ID=NE0422025&VA=Y&...>.

"Poliomyelitis: A Brief History." Welcome to Cloudnet! Web. 2 Feb. 2009. <http://www.cloudnet.com/~edrbsass/poliohistory.htm>.

"Red Cloud, Bozeman Trail." Stage Coach - American Western History Museums - Bronze Stagecoach. American Western History Museum, 1999. Web. 8 Dec. 2008. <http://www.linecamp.com/museums/american-west/western_names/red_cloud/red_cloud.html>.

"Red Cloud, Nebraska - Travel, Lodging, Events, Attractions, Recreation." Travel, Lodging, Attractions, Events, Recreation. Web. 1 Feb. 2009. <http://www.lasr.net/travel/city.php?City_ID=NE0422025>.

"Red Cloud." Travel and History. Web. 25 Feb. 2009. <http://www.u-s-history.com/pages/h3756.html>.

"The Red Cloud Opera House." The Red Cloud Opera House - Atractions in Red Cloud, Nebraska - Travel, Lodging, Events, Recreation. Web. 1 Feb. 2009. <http://www.lasr.net/travel/city.php?RedCloud&Nebraska&City_ID=NE0422025&VA=Y&...>.

"Sputnik: 50 Years Ago." Don P. Mitchell: Soviet Space, Venus, Tesla, Computers, Graphics, Science. Web. 9 Jan. 2009. <http://www.mentallandscape.com/S_Sputnik.htm>.

Stephens, Andy. "Feature - Jan. 23, 1949: Snowbound in the Heartland." 11th Wing, Bolling Air Force Base - Home. 24 Jan. 2007. Web. 2 Jan. 2009. <http://www.bolling.af.mil/news/story.asp?id=123038650>.

Stephens, Mitchell. "History of Television - Grolier Encyclopedia." New York University. Web. 5 Jan. 2009. <http://www.nyu.edu/classes/stephens/History%20of%20Television%20page.htm>.

"Treaty of Fort Laramie 1868." Republic of Lakotah - Mitakuye Oya sin. 28 Dec. 2008. Web. 25 Feb. 2009. <http://www.republicoflakotah.com/?tag=lakotah-sioux-cheif-red-cloud>.

Underwood, Todd. "The Oregon Trail." Frontier Trails of The Old West. AtJeu Publishing. Web. 24 June 2009. <http://www.frontiertrails.com/oldwest/oregontrail.htm>.

Webster's New World Dictionary of the American Language. College ed. Cleveland and New York: The World Company, 1960. Print.

"Zebulon Pike Educational Material - Pike National Trail Association and Membership. Web. 1 Feb. 2009. <http://zebulonpike.org/zebulon-pike-route-maps.htm>.

CPSIA information can be obtained at www.ICGtesting.com
Printed in the USA
BVOW04s1837130214

344870BV00001B/16/P